5000 GERMAN WORDS

**Essential Vocabulary
for Examinations**

COLLINS GEM

5000 GERMAN WORDS

Barbara I. Christie

HarperCollins*Publishers*

first published in this edition 1991

© William Collins Sons & Co. Ltd. 1979
© HarperCollins Publishers 1991

latest reprint 1993

ISBN 0 00 459322 7

*Printed in Great Britain by
HarperCollins Manufacturing, Glasgow*

Whether you are revising for school exams or whether, as an adult user, you want to brush up your German vocabulary, this book offers you the information you require in a helpful and accessible format.

The main part of the book comprises 50 topics, covering such common vocabulary areas as ANIMALS, GREETINGS, HEALTH, SHOPPING and the WEATHER. These are given in alphabetical order, in double-page spreads.

Vocabulary within each topic is divided into the relevant nouns for that topic, in alphabetical order, followed by appropriate adjectives, verbs, example phrases and constructions. These build up a fuller picture of the topic in question, and will help you to produce the kind of sentences you need in everyday communication.

Nouns are grouped by gender, which makes it easier to remember if they are masculine, feminine or neuter. In addition, vocabulary within each topic is graded, so that you can choose what to cover according to your particular requirements. ESSENTIAL vocabulary includes the basics for communication on a given topic, IMPORTANT items expand on this, and USEFUL material increases the depth with which you will be able to express yourself on the topic in question.

This arrangement is particularly helpful for GCSE revision, since ESSENTIAL vocabulary covers the minimum requirements for GCSE at Basic level. If in addition you learn the IMPORTANT vocabulary, you will have covered everything you need for GCSE at Higher level.

All plurals have been included in the text with the exception of feminine nouns ending in -in (which regularly become -innen in the plural) and those forms, of whatever gender, which have the same form in both singular and plural.

Nouns derived from adjectives take the form:

Zollbeamte(r), -n customs officer
Alte(r), -n old man/woman

This indicates that the noun ending depends on the article being used. Thus:

masculine singular	**der Zollbeamte**
	ein Zollbeamter
masculine plural	**die Zollbeamten**
	Zollbeamte
feminine singular	**die Zollbeamte**
	eine Zollbeamte
feminine plural	**die Zollbeamten**
	Zollbeamte

Two symbols are used in the topics sections. The book symbol ⌂ shows words which you must be able to recognize without necessarily being able to use yourself. This symbol is used to mark vocabulary in both the ESSENTIAL and IMPORTANT categories but all GCSE students at Higher level must treat items of ESSENTIAL vocabulary so marked as if they had no symbol: you must know them actively, not just for comprehension.

The arrow symbol ⇨ alerts you to the fact that the word so marked can have another meaning, either in the same topic or in a completely different one. There is a list of these words at the end of the book, entitled HOMONYMS.

Of course a knowledge of German doesn't begin and end with memorizing individual words, and this is where the phrases and idioms given at the bottom of the page come into their own. These are just the sorts of expressions you will be likely to hear and will want to produce for yourself. It will help you to become familiar with them if you practise them in different ways: try them out as questions and negatives as well as statements, use them in different persons of the verb, and in different tenses.

The second section of the book groups words according to part of speech — adjective, noun, verb etc — to provide you with a useful checklist. This includes words which can be used with most or even all the topics — the type of vocabulary which you will come across in everyday situations and which is not confined to one particular topic.

Finally, there is an English index which covers all the ESSENTIAL and IMPORTANT nouns given under the topic headings.

ABBREVIATIONS

acc	accusative	*jdn*	jemanden
adj	adjective	*m*	masculine
adv	adverb	*n*	noun
conj	conjunction	*nt*	neuter
dat	dative	*pl*	plural
etw	etwas	*prep*	preposition
f	feminine	*sb*	somebody
gen	genitive	*sth*	something
jdm	jemandem		

CONTENTS

ESSENTIAL WORDS (m)	
der Ausgang, ¨-e	way out, exit
der Ausstieg, -e 🔲	exit
der Eingang, ¨-e	entrance
der Fahrgast, ¨-e 🔲	passenger
der Fahrkartenschalter	ticket office
der Fahrplan, ¨-e	timetable
der Fallschirm, -e	parachute
die Ferien (pl)	holiday
der Flug, ¨-e	flight
der Fluggast, ¨-e	airline passenger
der Flughafen, ¨-	airport
der Flugplatz, ¨-e	airfield; airport
der Flugpreis, -e	(air) fare
der Gepäckträger ◇	porter
der Geschäftsmann,	
(-leute)	businessman
der Koffer	case, suitcase
der Kofferkuli, -s	luggage trolley
der Nichtraucher	non-smoker
der Notausgang, ¨-e 🔲	emergency exit
der Paß ◇, -sse	passport
der Passagier, -e	passenger
der Raucher	smoker
Reisende(r), -n	traveller
der Reisepaß, ¨-sse	passport
der Steward, -s	steward
der Tourist, -en	tourist
der Urlaub	holiday(s)
der Urlauber	holiday-maker
der Zoll	customs; duty
der Zuschlag, ¨-e	extra charge

ESSENTIAL WORDS (f)	
die Ankunft, ¨e 📖	arrival
die Auskunft ◇, ¨e 📖	information; information desk
die (einfache) Fahrkarte, -n	(single) ticket
die Flugkarte, -n	(plane) ticket
die Gepäckaufbewahrung 📖	left luggage office
die Luft	air
die Maschine ◇, -n 📖	plane
die Nummer, -n	number
die Reservierung, -en	booking, reservation
die Richtung, -en	direction
die Rückfahrkarte, -n	return (ticket)
die Stewardeß, -essen	air hostess
die Tasche ◇, -n	bag
die Toilette, -n	toilet
die Touristin	tourist
die Uhr ◇, -en	clock; time
die Urlauberin	holiday-maker

ESSENTIAL WORDS (nt)	
das Flie...	flying
das F... ...s	plane, aeroplane
d... ...	lost property office
	luggage
...flugzeug, -e	airliner
	left luggage locker
	taxi
	(plane) ticket

...ket lösen to buy a (plane) ticket
...n/bestätigen to book/confirm a

...ach Köln a return to Cologne
...ck; ich packe aus I unpack
...y; wir fliegen ab we fly off
... to catch; verpassen to miss

IMPORTANT WORDS (m)

der Abflug, ⁼e ⌑	takeoff, departure
der Bord, ◇, -e	board
der Dienst, -e	service
der Fahrausweis, -e ⌑	ticket
der Fahrschein, -e	ticket
der Hubschrauber	helicopter
der Jumbo-Jet, -s	jumbo jet
der Kontrollturm, ⁼e	control tower
der Pilot, -en	pilot
der Sicherheitsgurt, ⁼e ⌑	seat belt
der Start, -s	takeoff
der Terminal, -s	(air) terminal
Zollbeamte(r), -n	customs officer

IMPORTANT WORDS (f)

die Ausreise, -n	departure (*from country*)
die Bordkarte, -n	boarding card
die Geschwindigkeit, -en	speed
die Landung, -en	landing
die Startbahn, -en	runway
die Verbindung, -en	connection
die Verspätung, -en	delay
die Zollkontrolle	customs control *or* check

IMPORTANT WORDS (nt)

das zollfreie Geschäft, -n -e	duty-free shop
das Reisebüro, -s	travel agent's
das Reiseziel, ◇, -e	destination

starten to take off; **beim Start** during the takeoff
an Bord on board; **luftkrank** airsick
schnallen Sie sich bitte an, "bitte anschnallen" please
    fasten your seat belts
wir haben eine Flughöhe von . . . we are flying at a height
    of . . .
landen to land; **verspätet** delayed, late

USEFUL WORDS (m)

der Abstieg	descent
der Absturz, ⸚e	plane crash
der Anhänger ◇	label, tag
der Aufkleber	sticker, label
der Flügel ◇	wing
der Fluglotse, -n	air traffic controller

USEFUL WORDS (f)

die Besatzung, -en	crew
die Einreisekarte, -n	landing card
die Höhe	height, altitude
die Landebahn, -en	runway
die Luftverkehrsgesell-	
schaft, -en	airline
die Rollbahn, -en	runway
die Rolltreppe, -n	escalator
die Schallmauer	sound barrier
die Turbulenz	turbulence
die Zwischenlandung, -en	stopover

USEFUL WORDS (nt)

das Armaturenbrett ◇	instrument panel
das Bodenpersonal	ground staff
das Düsenflugzeug, -e	jet plane

einen Zuschlag zahlen to pay a supplement
zuschlagpflichtig subject to an extra charge
gültig valid
durch den Zoll gehen to go through customs
verzollen to pay duty on
haben Sie etwas zu verzollen? do you have anything to declare?
nichts zu verzollen nothing to declare
zollfrei duty-free

ESSENTIAL WORDS (m)

der Elefant, -en	elephant
der Fisch, -e	fish
der Hals, ⸚e	neck; throat
der Hund, -e	dog
der Tiergarten, ⸚	zoo, zoological park
der Versuch ◇, -e	experiment
der Zoo, -s	zoo

IMPORTANT WORDS (m)

der Affe, -n ▢	monkey
der Bär, -en	bear
der Bock, ⸚e	buck, ram
der Hamster, -	hamster
der Huf, -e	hoof
der Löwe, -n ▢	lion
der Schwanz, ⸚e	tail
der Tiger, -	tiger
der Wolf, ⸚e	wolf

ESSENTIAL WORDS (f)

die Katze, -n	cat
die Tierhandlung, -en	pet shop

IMPORTANT WORDS (f)

die Giraffe, -n	giraffe
die Hundehütte, -n	kennel
die Kuh, ⸚e	cow
die Löwin ▢	lioness
die Maus, Mäuse	mouse
die Ratte, -n	rat
die Schlange ◇, -n ▢	snake
die Tigerin	tigress

laufen to run; **hüpfen** to hop
springen to jump; **kriechen** to slither, crawl

ESSENTIAL WORDS (nt)	
das Bein, -e	leg
das Haar, -e	hair
das Haustier, -e	pet
die Jungen (*pl*)	young
das Ohr, -en	ear
das Tier, -e	animal

IMPORTANT WORDS (nt)	
das Horn, ⁻er	horn
das Kamel, -e	camel
das Känguruh, -s	kangaroo
das Kaninchen, -	rabbit
das Krokodil, -e	crocodile
das Pferd, -e	horse
das Pony ⬦**, -s**	pony
das Rhinozeros, -se	rhinoceros
das Schaf, -e	sheep
das Schwein, -e	pig
das Zebra, -s	zebra

wir haben keine Haustiere we don't have any pets
zahm tame; **wild** wild; **gehorsam** obedient
füttern to feed; **fressen** to eat
trinken to drink
schlafen to sleep
bellen to bark; **miauen** to miaow
knurren to growl; **schnurren** to purr
beißen to bite; **kratzen** to scratch
ich habe Angst vor Hunden I'm afraid of dogs

USEFUL WORDS *(m)*

der Beutel	pouch (*of kangaroo*)
der Bulle, -n	bull
der Eisbär, -en	polar bear
der Esel	donkey
der Frosch, ̈e	frog
der Fuchs, ̈e	fox
der Hase, -n	hare
der Hirsch, -e	stag
der Höcker	hump (*of camel*)
der Igel	hedgehog
der Kater	tomcat
der Maulwurf, ̈e	mole
der Ochse, -n	ox
der Panzer ⟡	shell (*of tortoise*)
der Pelz, -e	fur
der Rüssel	snout (*of pig*); trunk (*of elephant*)
der Seehund, -e	seal
der Stachel, -n	spine (*of hedgehog*)
der Stier, -e	bull
der Stoßzahn, ̈e	tusk
der Streifen	stripe (*of zebra*)
der Wal(fisch), -e	whale
der Ziegenbock, ̈e	billy goat

jagen to hunt; to shoot
zu Pferd on horseback
reiten gehen to go riding
auf die Fuchsjagd gehen to go fox-hunting
"Warnung vor dem Hunde" "beware of the dog"
der Hund wedelt mit dem Schwanz the dog wags its tail
die Katze streicheln to stroke the cat

USEFUL WORDS (f)

die Falle, -n	trap
die Fledermaus, (-mäuse)	bat
die Gespenstheuschrecke, -n	stick insect
die Kralle, -n	claw; talon
die Kröte, -n	toad
die Mähne, -n	mane
die Natter, -n	adder
die Pfote, -n	paw (*small*)
die Pranke, -n	paw (*large*)
die Ringelnatter	grass snake
die Robbe, -n	seal
die Schildkröte, -n	tortoise
die Schnauze, -n	snout, muzzle
die Tatze, -n	paw
die Ziege, -n	goat, nanny goat

USEFUL WORDS (nt)

das Eichhörnchen	squirrel
das Fell, -e	coat, fur
das Geweih	antlers (*pl*)
das Hufeisen	horseshoe
das Maul, Mäuler	mouth
das Maultier, -e	mule
das Meerschweinchen	guinea pig
das Merkmal, -e	characteristic
das Nashorn, ̈-er	rhinoceros
das Nilpferd, -e	hippopotamus
das Reh, -e	roe deer

ein Tier freilassen to set an animal free

... Löwe ist aus dem Zoo entlaufen a lion has escaped ... zoo

... gehen to be caught in a trap

ESSENTIAL + IMPORTANT WORDS (m)

der Gang ⟡, ⁼e	gear
der Gepäckträger ⟡	luggage carrier
der Motorradfahrer	motorcyclist
der Radfahrer	cyclist
der Rad(fahr)weg, -e	cycle track or path
der Radsport	cycling
der Reifen	tyre
der Sattel, ⁼	saddle, seat

ESSENTIAL + IMPORTANT WORDS (f)

die Achtung	attention
die Bahn, -en	road, way; (cycle) lane
die Bremse, -n	brake
die Ecke, -n	corner
die Fahrradlampe, -n	cycle lamp
die Gefahr, -en ▢	danger, risk
die Geschwindigkeit, -en	speed
die Hauptstraße, -n	main street, main road
die Kette, -n	chain
die Klingel, -n	bell
die Lampe, -n	lamp
die Nebenstraße, -n	side street
die Pumpe, -n	pump
die Radfahrerin	cyclist
die Reifenpanne, -n	puncture
die Reparatur, -en	repair; repairing

mit dem (Fahr)rad fahren to cycle
mit dem Rad in die Stadt fahren to cycle into town
er kam mit dem Rad he came on his bike, he came by bike
"Radfahren verboten" "cycling prohibited"
Radsport betreiben to go in for cycling
aufsteigen to get on; absteigen to get off
bergauf uphill; bergab downhill
klingeln to ring one's bell
schalten to change gear

ESSENTIAL WORDS (nt)

das Fahrrad, ⸚er	bicycle
das Hinterrad, ⸚er	back wheel
das Motorrad, ⸚er	motorbike, motorcycle
das Pedal, -e	pedal
das Rad ⬦, ⸚er	wheel; bike
das Radfahren	cycling
das Vorderrad, ⸚er	front wheel

USEFUL WORDS (m)

der Dynamo, -s	dynamo
der Helm, -e	helmet
der Korb, ⸚e	pannier; basket
der Rückstrahler	reflector
der Schmutzfänger	mud flap

USEFUL WORDS (f)

die Lenkstange, -n	handlebars
die Querstange, -n	crossbar
die Satteltasche, -n	saddlebag, pannier
die Speiche, -n	spoke
die Steigung, -en	gradient
die Straßenverkehrs-ordnung	the Highway Code

USEFUL WORDS (nt)

das Flickzeug, -e	puncture repair kit
das Katzenauge, -n	rear light; reflector; cat's eye
das Schutzblech, -e	mudguard

bremsen to brake; **reparieren** to repair
ein Le **Platten haben** to have a flat tyre
from the erst; **kaputt** broken, done
in eine Falle ᵗᵉn to mend the puncture
ᵘumpen to blow up the tyres
rostig rusty; **Leucht-** fluorescent

ESSENTIAL + IMPORTANT WORDS (m)

der Flamingo, -s	flamingo
der Hahn ♢, ⁼e	cock
der Himmel	sky
der Käfig, -e	cage
der Kanarienvogel, ⁼	canary
der Kuckuck, -e	cuckoo
der Pinguin, -e	penguin
der Schwan, ⁼e	swan
der Storch, ⁼e	stork
der Truthahn, ⁼e	turkey
der Vogel, ⁼	bird
der Wellensittich, -e	budgie, budgerigar

ESSENTIAL + IMPORTANT WORDS (f)

die Ente, -n	duck
die Feder ♢, -n	feather
die Gans, ⁼e	goose
die Henne, -n	hen
die Luft	air
die Nachtigall, -en	nightingale

ESSENTIAL + IMPORTANT WORDS (nt)

das Huhn, ⁼er	hen, fowl
das Nest, -er	nest
das Rotkehlchen	robin (redbreast)
das *or* der (Vogel)bauer ♢ ▢	birdcage

fliegen to fly; **abfliegen** to fly away
ein Nest bauen to build a nest; **nisten** to nest
Eier legen to lay eggs
singen to sing
pfeifen to whistle
zwitschern to twitter
Lärm machen to make a noise

USEFUL WORDS (m)

der Adler	eagle
der Eisvogel, ⁝	kingfisher
der Falke, -n	falcon
der Fasan, -e(n)	pheasant
der Fink, -en	finch
der Flügel ◊	wing
der Geier	vulture
der Habicht, -e	hawk
der Hirtenstar, -s	mynah bird
der Papagei, -en	parrot
der Pfau, -en	peacock
der Puter	turkey(-cock)
der Rabe, -n	raven
der Schnabel, ⁝	beak, bill
der Sittich, -e	parakeet
der Spatz, -en	sparrow
der Specht, -e	woodpecker
der Sperling, -e	sparrow
der Star ◊, -e	starling
der Strauß ◊, -e	ostrich
der Zaunkönig, -e	wren

USEFUL WORDS (f)

die Amsel, -n	blackbird
die Blaumeise, -n	bluetit
die Dohle, -n	jackdaw
die Drossel, -n	thrush
die Elster, -n	magpie
die Eule, -n	owl
die Krähe, -n	crow
die Lerche, -n	lark
die Möwe, -n	seagull
die Saatkrähe, -n	rook
die Schwalbe, -n	swallow
die Taube, -n	dove; pigeon

The BODY

ESSENTIAL WORDS (m)

der Arm, -e	arm
der Bauch, Bäuche	stomach
der Finger	finger
der Fuß, ⁻e	foot
der Hals, ⁻e	neck; throat
der Kopf, ⁻	head
der Magen, - *or* ⁻	stomach
der Mund, ⁻er	mouth
der Rücken	back
der Zahn, ⁻e	tooth

ESSENTIAL WORDS (f)

die Bewegung, -en □	movement, motion
die Hand, ⁻e	hand
die Nase, -n	nose
die Seite ◇, -n	side

ESSENTIAL WORDS (nt)

das Auge, -n	eye
das Bein, -e	leg
das Fleisch ◇	flesh
das Gesicht, -er	face
das Haar, -e	hair
das Ohr, -en	ear

ich habe mir den Arm/das Bein gebrochen I've broken my arm/leg

mein Arm/Bein tut weh my arm/leg hurts

zu Fuß on foot

barfuß gehen to go *or* walk barefoot

von Kopf bis Fuß from head to foot, from top to toe

den Kopf schütteln to shake one's head

mit den Kopf nicken to nod one's head

jdm die Hand geben to shake hands with sb

(mit der Hand) winken to wave

auf etwas zeigen to point to something

IMPORTANT WORDS (m)	
der Atem	breath
der Daumen	thumb
der Körper	body
der Körperteil, -e	part of the body
der Zeigefinger	forefinger, index finger

IMPORTANT WORDS (f)	
die Lippe, -n	lip
die Schulter, -n	shoulder
die Stimme, -n	voice
die Zunge, -n	tongue

IMPORTANT WORDS (nt)	
das Blut	blood
das Herz, -en	heart
das Knie	knee

sehen to see; **hören** to hear
fühlen to feel; **riechen** to smell
tasten to touch; **schmecken** to taste
sich die Nase putzen to blow one's nose
jdm auf die Schulter klopfen to tap sb on the shoulder
sein Herz klopfte his heart was beating
die linke/rechte Körperseite the lefthand/righthand side of the body
neben mir at my side
eine leise/laute Stimme haben to have a soft/loud voice
leise/laut sprechen to speak softly/loudly
ich lasse mir die Haare schneiden I'm having my hair cut
auf den Knien on one's knees
stehen to stand; **sitzen** to sit
sich legen to lie down; **knien** to kneel (down)
bewegen to move (*part of the body*)
sich bewegen to move (*one's self*)

USEFUL WORDS (m)

der Ell(en)bogen	elbow
der (Fuß)knöchel	ankle
der Hintern	bottom
der Kiefer ⇨	jaw
der Knöchel	knuckle; ankle
der Knochen	bone
der Muskel, -n	muscle
der Nacken	nape of the neck
der Nagel, ⸚	nail
der Nerv, -en	nerve
der Schenkel	thigh

USEFUL WORDS (nt)

das (Augen)lid, -er	eyelid
das Blutgefäß, -e	blood vessel
das Gehirn, -e	brain
das Gelenk, -e	joint
das Genick, -e	nape of the neck
das Glied, -er	limb
das Handgelenk, -e	wrist
das Kinn, -e	chin
die Maße (pl)	measurements
das Rückgrat, -e	spine
das Skelett, -e	skeleton

ich habe mir den Knöchel verstaucht I've sprained my ankle
biegen to bend; **strecken** to stretch
stürzen to fall
verletzen, verwu iden to injure
müde tired
fit; unfit unfit
ich ruhe mich aus I'm resting *or* having a rest
taub deaf; **blind** blind; **stumm** dumb
körperbehindert physically handicapped
geistig behindert mentally handicapped

> *USEFUL WORDS (f)*

die Ader, -n	vein
die Arterie, -n	artery
die Augenbraue, -n	eyebrow
die (Augen)wimper, -n	eyelash
die Brust, ⁻e	breast; chest
die Büste, -n	bust
die Faust, Fäuste	fist
die Ferse, -n	heel
die Figur, -en	figure
die Form, -en	shape, figure
die Fußsohle, -n	sole of the foot
die Gestalt, -en	figure, form, shape
die Geste, -n	gesture
die Haut	skin
die Hüfte, -n	hip
die Kehle, -n	throat
die Leber, -n	liver
die Lunge, -n	lung
die Niere, -n	kidney
die Pupille, -n	pupil (*of eye*)
die Rippe, -n	rib
die Schläfe, -n	temple
die Schlagader, -n	artery
die Stirn, -en	forehead
die Taille, -n	waist
die Wade, -n	calf (*of leg*)
die Wange, -n	cheek
die Zehe, -n	toe
die große Zehe, -n -n	big toe

Brustumfang (*m*) bust *or* chest measurement
Hüftweite (*f*) hip measurement
Taillenweite (*f*) waist measurement

The CALENDAR

THE SEASONS

der Frühling	spring
der Sommer	summer
der Herbst	autumn
der Winter	winter

im Frühling/Sommer/Herbst/Winter in spring/summer/
autumn/winter

THE MONTHS

Januar	January	**Juli**	July
Februar	February	**August**	August
März	March	**September**	September
April	April	**Oktober**	October
Mai	May	**November**	November
Juni	June	**Dezember**	December

im September *etc* in September *etc*
der erste April April Fools' Day
der erste Mai May Day
der fünfte November (*Tag der Pulververschwörung in
England*) Guy Fawkes Night

THE DAYS OF THE WEEK

Montag	Monday
Dienstag	Tuesday
Mittwoch	Wednesday
Donnerstag	Thursday
Freitag	Friday
Samstag } **Sonnabend** }	Saturday
Sonntag	Sunday

Freitags *etc* on Fridays *etc*
am Freitag *etc* on Friday *etc*
nächsten/letzten Freitag *etc* next/last Friday *etc*
am nächsten Freitag *etc* the following Friday *etc*

THE CALENDAR

Advent (*m*) Advent
der Adventskranz Advent wreath
Allerheiligen (*nt*) All Saints' Day
der Abend vor Allerheiligen Hallowe'en
Allerseelen (*nt*) All Souls' Day
Aschermittwoch (*m*) Ash Wednesday
Dreikönigfest (*nt*) Epiphany, Twelfth Night
Faschingszeit (*f*) the Fasching festival, carnival time
Fastenzeit (*f*) Lent
Fastnacht (*f*) Shrove Tuesday
Heiliger Abend, Heiligabend (*m*) Christmas Eve
Karfreitag (*m*) Good Friday
Neujahr (*nt*) New Year
Neujahrstag (*m*) New Year's Day
Ostern (*nt*) Easter
Ostersonntag (*m*) Easter Sunday
Palmsonntag (*m*) Palm Sunday
Passahfest (*nt*) (Feast of the) Passover
Pfingsten (*nt*) Whitsun
Silvesmontag (*m*) Whit Monday
Silvester, Sylvester (*nt*) New Year's Eve, Hogmanay
Silvesterabend (*m*) New Year's Eve, Hogmanay
Valentinstag (*m*) St Valentine's Day
der Valentinsgruß Valentine card
Weihnachten (*pl*) Christmas
Weihnachtsabend (*m*) Christmas Eve
Weihnachtstag (*m*) Christmas Day
zweiter Weihnachtstag (*m*) Boxing Day
die Weihnachtskarte Christmas card

zu Weihnachten/Ostern/Pfingsten at Christmas/Easter/
Whitsun

SPECIAL EVENTS	
die Beerdigung, -en	funeral, burial
die Bescherung	distribution of Christmas presents
der Feiertag, -e	holiday
das Festival, -s	festival
der Festtag, -e	holiday
das Feuer im Freien	bonfire
das Feuerwerk, -e	firework display
der Feuerwerkskörper	firework
der Friedhof, -̈e	cemetery, graveyard
der Geburstag, -e	birthday
das Geschenk, -e	present
die Heirat, -en	marriage
der Hochzeitstag, -e	wedding day
die Jahreszeit, -en	season
der Kalender	calendar
das Konfetti	confetti
der geschmückte Plattformwagen	decorated float
der Wochentag, -e	weekday
der Tanz, -̈e and **Tanzabend**	dance
die Taufe	christening, baptism
der Tod, -e	death
der Zirkus, -se	circus

seinen Geburtstag feiern to celebrate one's birthday
der Silvestertanz New Year's Eve dance
jemandem ein Geschenk machen to give somebody a present
Feuerwerk abbrennen to set off fireworks
ihr dritte Hochzeitstag their second (wedding) anniversary
beglückwünschen (zu) to congratulate (on)
wünschen to wish
(herzlich) Willkommen! you are (very) welcome!
in Trauer in mourning
den wievielten haben wir heute? what is today's date?

SPECIAL EVENTS

die Blaskapelle, -n	brass band
das Fest, -e	fête; feast (day)
die Flitterwochen (pl)	honeymoon (time)
das Folksongfestival	folk music festival
die Geburt, -en	birth
die Hochzeit, -en	wedding
die Hochzeitsreise, -n	honeymoon (journey)
der Jahrmarkt, ⁻e	fair
die Messe ◇, -n	(commercial) fair
der Namenstag, -e	saint's day
das Neujahrsgeschenk	New Year's gift, Christmas box
der Ruhestand	retirement
der Rummelplatz, ⁻e	fairground
die Trauung, -en	wedding ceremony
die Verabredung, -en	date (with sb)
die Verlobung, -en	engagement
die Zeremonie, -n	ceremony

auf eine or **zu einer Hochzeit gehen** to go to a wedding
silberne/goldene/diamantene Hochzeit silver/golden/ diamond wedding
in den Ruhestand treten to retire, go into retirement
die Stadt mit Blumen ausschmücken to decorate the town with flowers
die ganze Stadt war beflaggt there were flags out all over town
gute Vorsätze fassen to make good resolutions
beerdigen to bury

ESSENTIAL WORDS (m)

der Camper	camper (*person*)
der Campingplatz, ¨-e	camp site
der Löffel	spoon
der Rucksack, ¨-e	backpack, rucksack
der Schlafsack, ¨-e	sleeping bag
der Teller	plate
der Urlaub	holiday(s)
der Wohnwagen	caravan
der Zuschlag, ¨-e	extra charge

ESSENTIAL WORDS (f)

die Anmeldung ◇ 🗀	registration
die Camperin	camper (*person*)
die Dusche, -n	shower
die Gabel, -n	fork
die Landkarte, -n	map
die Lufte, ¨-e	air
die Nacht, ¨-e	night
die Sache, -n	thing
die Tasse, -n	cup
die Toilette, -n	toilet
die Übernachtung, -en	overnight stay
die Waschmaschine, -n	washing machine

ESSENTIAL WORDS (nt)

das Camping	camping
das Essen ◇	food; meal
das Glas, ¨-er	glass
das Messer	knife
das (Trink)wasser	(drinking) water
das Zelt, -e	tent

Camping machen to go camping
ein Zelt aufbauen *or* **aufschlagen** to pitch a tent
ein Zelt abbauen to take down a tent
"Zelten verboten!" "no camping"

IMPORTANT + USEFUL WORDS (m)

der Aufenthalt, -e	stay
der Campingkocher	camping stove
der Dosenöffner	tin-opener
der Feuerlöscher 🕮	fire extinguisher
der Klappstuhl, ⸚e	folding chair
der Klapptisch, -e	folding table
der Korkenzieher	corkscrew
der Liegestuhl, ⸚e	deck chair
der Mülleimer	dustbin
der Rasierapparat, -e	razor
der Schatten	shade; shadow
der Waschraum, (-räume)	washroom
der Zeltboden, ⸚	ground sheet
der Zimmernachweis 🕮	accommodation office

IMPORTANT + USEFUL WORDS (f)

die Büchse ⇩, -n	tin, can; box
die Luftmatratze, -n	lilo, air bed
die Münzwäscherei	launderette
die Nachtruhe 🕮	lights-out
die Ruhe ⇩	peace; rest
die Taschenlampe, -n	torch
die Unterkunft, ⸚e	accommodation
die Veranstaltung, -en 🕮	organization
die Wäsche	washing (*things*)
die Wäscherei	laundry (*place*)

IMPORTANT + USEFUL WORDS (nt)

das Campinggas	camping gas
das Fahrzeug, -e 🕮	vehicle
das Geschirr ⇩	dishes, crockery; pots and pans
das Lagerfeuer	campfire
das Schwarze Brett 🕮	notice board
das Streichholz, ⸚er	match
das Waschpulver	washing powder, detergent

ESSENTIAL WORDS (m)	
der **Arbeiter**	worker, labourer
Arbeitslose(r)	unemployed man/woman
der **Arzt, Ärzte**	doctor
der **Briefträger**	postman
der **Chef, -s** □	boss, head
der **Geschäftsmann,**	businessman
(-leute)	
Handlungsreisende(r), -n	travelling salesman/-woman
der **Job, -s**	(spare time) job
der **Koch, ⁻e**	cook
der **Last(kraft)wagenfahrer;**	
der **LKW-Fahrer**	lorry driver
der **Lehrer**	teacher
der **Milchmann, ⁻er**	milkman
der **Polizist, -en**	policeman
der **Taxifahrer**	taxi driver
der **Techniker**	technician

ESSENTIAL WORDS (f)	
die **Arbeit** ◊, **-en**	work; job
die **Arbeiterin**	worker
die **Ärztin**	doctor
die **Bank** ◊, **-en**	bank
die **Bezahlung, -en**	payment
die **Chefin** □	boss
die **Empfangsdame, -n** □	receptionist
die **Fabrik, -en**	factory
die **Geschäftsreise, -n**	business trip
die **Industrie, -n**	industry
die **Köchin**	cook
die **Krankenschwester, -n**	nurse
die **Lehrerin**	teacher
die **Polizistin**	policewoman
die **Stewardeß, -essen**	air hostess

ESSENTIAL WORDS (*nt*)

das Büro, -s   office
das Geschäft ⇔, **-e**   business, trade; shop

arbeiten to work; **bei X arbeiten** to work at X's
interessant interesting; **langweilig** boring
mit der Arbeit anfangen, zu arbeiten beginnen to start work, get down to work
berufstätig sein to be employed
arbeitslos sein to be out of work, be unemployed
arbeitslos werden to be made redundant
Arbeitslosengeld beziehen to be on the dole
seine Stelle verlieren to lose one's job
entlassen to dismiss
entlassen werden to be sacked, get the sack
jobben to do odd jobs
eine Stelle suchen to look for a job
"Stellenangebote" "situations vacant"
fest permanent; **vorübergehend** temporary
ganztags full-time; **stundenweise** part-time
sich um eine Stelle bewerben to apply for a job
eine Stelle antreten to start a new job
verdienen to earn
200 Pfund in der Woche verdienen to earn £200 per week
sparen für + *acc* to save up for
was sind Sie von Beruf? what is your job?
ich bin Elektriker (von Beruf) I am an electrician (to trade)
ehrgeizig ambitious
selbstständig self-employed
ich möchte Sekretärin werden I'd like to be a secretary
sein eigenes Geschäft haben to have one's own shop
eine Geschäftsreise machen to be away on business
streiken to strike, be on strike

das V.
das V.

IMPORTANT WORDS (m)	
Angestellte(r), -n	employee
der Ansager 🕮	announcer
der Apotheker	chemist
der Arbeitslohn, ⸚e 🕮	wages, pay
der Architekt, -en	architect
der Astronaut, -en	astronaut
Beamte(r)	official
der Beruf, -e	profession, occupation
der Betrieb, ⋄ -e 🕮	firm, concern
der Bibliothekar, -e	librarian
der Boß, -sse	boss
Büroangestellte(r), -n	office worker, clerk
der Elektriker	electrician
der Feuerwehrmann, (-männer)	fireman
der Fotograf, -en	photographer
der Friseur, -e	hairdresser
der Gastarbeiter	foreign (guest) worker
der Geschäftsführer	executive; manager
der Ingenieur, -e	engineer
der Journalist, -en	journalist
der Lehrling, -e	apprentice, trainee
der Lohn, ⸚e 🕮	wages, pay
der Maler	painter
der Mechaniker	mechanic
der Pilot, -en	pilot
der Poet, -en	poet
der Politiker	politician
der Präsident, -en	president
der Premierminister	prime minister, premier
der Priester	priest
der Reporter	reporter
der Sekretär ⋄, -e	secretary
Staatsbeamte(r), -n	civil servant
der Star ⋄, -s	star
der Tierarzt, ⸚e	veterinary surgeon, vet
der Verkäufer	salesman, shop assistant

IMPORTANT WORDS (f)

die Ansagerin ⌑	announcer
die Architektin	architect
die Astronautin	astronaut
die Berufsberatung	careers *or* vocational guidance
die Bibliothekarin	librarian
die Firma, Firmen	firm, company
die Friseuse, -n	hairdresser
die Geschäftsführerin	executive; manageress
die Gesellschaft, -en	company
die Journalistin	journalist
die Lehrzeit, -en	apprenticeship
die Maschinenschreiberin	typist
die Putzfrau, -en	cleaner, cleaning woman
die Sekretärin	secretary
die Stelle ⇨, -n	job, post
die Tierärztin	veterinary surgeon, vet
die Verkäuferin	salesgirl, shop assistant
die Zukunft	future

IMPORTANT WORDS (nt)

das Einkommen	income
das Gehalt, ⸚er ⌑	salary
das Handwerk, -e	trade; craft
das Interview, -s	interview
das Kindermädchen	nanny
das Leben	life
das Mannequin, -s	model
das Ministerium, -ien	(government) ministry

USEFUL WORDS (m)	
Abgeordnete(r), -n	M.P., member of parliament
der Autor, -en	author
der Bauunternehmer	builder, building contractor
der Bergarbeiter	miner
der Betriebsleiter	managing director
der Chirurg, -en	surgeon
der Dichter	poet
der Dolmetscher	interpreter
der Fachmann, (-leute)	specialist, expert
der Forscher	researcher
der Gewerkschaftler	trade unionist
der Handel	commerce
der Hausmeister	caretaker; janitor
der Kameramann, (-männer)	cameraman
der Klempner	plumber
der König, -e	king
der Künstler	artist
der Leiter ⇔	leader, manager
der Matrose, -n	sailor
der Ministerpräsident, -en	prime minister, premier
der Modeschöpfer	fashion designer
der Mönch, -e	monk
der Pfarrer	minister, clergyman
der Produzent ⇔, -en	manufacturer; (film) producer
der Rechtsanwalt, ¨e	lawyer, solicitor
der Schneider	tailor
der Schriftsteller	writer
der Soldat, -en	soldier
der Steinmetz, -en	stonemason
der Tischler	joiner, carpenter
der Verleger	publisher
der Vertreter	representative, rep
Vorsitzende(r)	chairman/-woman
der Winzer	vinegrower, vineyard owner
der Wirtschaftsprüfer	chartered accountant
der Wissenschaftler	scientist

USEFUL WORDS (f)	
die **Absicht**, -en	intention, aim
die **Ausbildung**	training, education
die **Chirurgin**	surgeon
die **Dolmetscherin**	interpreter
die **Gewerkschaft**, -en	trade union
die **Königin**	queen
die **Künstlerin**	artist
die **Laufbahn**, -en	career
die **Lohnerhöhung**, -en	wage increase
die **Nonne**, -n	nun
die **Platzanweiserin**	usherette
die **Rechtsanwältin**	lawyer, solicitor
die **Schneiderin**	dressmaker
die **Sprechstundenhilfe**, -n	(medical) receptionist
die **Stenotypistin**	shorthand typist
die **Verwaltung**, -en	administration
die **Wissenschaftlerin**	scientist

ESSENTIAL WORDS (m)

der (Auto)fahrer	motorist, driver
der Führerschein, -e	driving licence
der Kilometer	kilometre
der Koffer	suitcase
der Lastkraftwagen (LKW) ▭	lorry, truck
der Lastwagenfahrer	lorry driver
der Liter	litre
der Parkplatz, ⁻e	parking space; car park
der Passagier, -e	passenger
der Personenkraftwagen (PKW) ▭	private car
der Polizist, -en	policeman
der Rasthof, ⁻e ▭	service station
der Rastplatz ⁻e ▭	lay-by
der Reifen	tyre
der Reifendruck	tyre pressure
der (Sport)wagen ⇨	(sports) car
der Weg ⇨, -e	road, way
der Wohnwagen	caravan

ESSENTIAL WORDS (nt)

das Auto, -s	car
das Benzin	petrol
das Dieselöl	diesel (oil)
das Gepäck	luggage
das Mietauto, -s	hired car
das Normal	2-star (petrol)
das Öl	oil
das Parkhaus, (-häuser)	(covered) multistorey car park
das Parken	parking
das Rad ⇨, ⁻er	wheel
das Selbsttanken	self-service petrol
das Straßenschild, -er	road sign
das Super	4-star (petrol)
das Wasser	water

ESSENTIAL WORDS (f)	

die **Achtung**	attention
die **Ampel, -n**	traffic lights
die **Ausfahrt, -en**	exit; drive; slip road
die **Autobahn, -en**	motorway
die **(Auto)fahrerin**	motorist, driver
die **Bahn, -en**	road, way; lane
die **Batterie, -n**	battery
die **Ecke, -n**	corner
die **Einbahnstraße, -n** ⌑	one-way street
die **Fahrt** ◇**, -en**	journey; trip; drive
die **Garage, -n**	garage
die **Hauptstraße, -n**	main road, main street
die **grüne Karte**	green card
die **Landkarte, -n**	map
die **Maschine** ◇**, -n** ⌑	engine
die **Polizei**	police
die **Polizistin**	policewoman
die **Raststätte, -n**	service area
die **Reise, -n**	journey
die **Reparatur, -en**	repair; repairing
die **(Reparatur)werkstatt, ¨en**	garage, workshop
die **Richtung, -en**	direction
die **Selbstbedienung (SB)** ⌑	self-service
die **Straße, -n**	street, road
die **Straßenkarte, -n**	road map, plan
die **Straßenverkehrsordnung**	the Highway Code
die **Tankstelle, -n**	petrol station, filling station, service station
die **Umleitung, -en**	diversion
die **Verkehrsampel, -n**	traffic lights
die **Vorfahrt** ⌑	right of way
die **Vorsicht**	caution, care
die **Warnung, -en** ⌑	warning
die **Werkstatt, ¨en**	garage, workshop

IMPORTANT WORDS (m)

der Abstand 🔲	distance
der Blinker	indicator
der Chauffeur, -e	chauffeur
der Dachgepäckträger	roof rack
der Fahrlehrer	driving instructor
der Fahrschüler	learner driver
der Fußgänger 🔲	pedestrian
der Gang ◇, ⁻e 🔲	gear
der Kofferraum, (-räume)	boot
der Mechaniker	mechanic; engineer
der Motorschaden	engine trouble
der Parkschein, -e	parking permit
der Rückspiegel	rear-view or driving mirror
der Scheinwerfer	headlight, headlamp
der Sicherheitsgurt, -e 🔲	seat belt
der Stau, -e 🔲	(traffic) jam
der Tod, -e	death
der Tramper	hitch-hiker
der Umweg, -e	detour
der Unfall, ⁻e	accident
der Verkehr	traffic
der Verkehrspolizist, -en	traffic warden
der Verkehrsunfall, ⁻e	road accident
Verletzte(r), -n	casualty
der Zusammenstoß, ⁻e	collision, crash

IMPORTANT WORDS (nt)

das Autobahndreieck, -e 🔲	motorway junction
das Autobahnkreuz, -e 🔲	motorway intersection
das Fahrzeug, -e 🔲	vehicle
das Firmenauto, -s	company car
das Parkverbot, -e	parking ban
das Reserverad, ⁻er	spare wheel
das Trampen	hitch-hiking
das Wohngebiet 🔲	built-up area

IMPORTANT WORDS (f)

die **Autoschlange**, -n 🔲	line of cars
die **Autowäsche**, -n 🔲	car wash
die **Bremse**, -n	brake
die **Fahrlehrerin**	driving instructress
die **Fahrprüfung**, -en	driving test
die **Fahrschule**, -n	driving school
die **Fahrschülerin**	learner driver
die **Fahrstunde**, -n	driving lesson
die **Gebühr**, -en 🔲	toll
die **Gefahr**, -en 🔲	danger, risk
die **Geldstrafe**, -n 🔲	fine
die **Geschwindigkeit**, -en	speed
die **Grenze**, -n	border, frontier
die **Hauptverkehrszeit**	rush hour
die **Kreuzung**, -en	crossroads
die **Kurve**, -n	bend, corner
die **Notbremsung**, -en	emergency stop
die **Panne**, -n	breakdown
die **Parkuhr**, -en	parking meter
die **Querstraße**, -n	junction, intersection
die **Reifenpanne**, -n	puncture
die **(Reise)route**, -n	route, itinerary
die **Ringstraße**, -n	ring road
die **Tiefgarage**, -n 🔲	underground garage
die **Verkehrspolizistin**	(female) traffic warden
die **Verkehrsstauung**, -en 🔲	traffic jam
die **Versicherung**	insurance
die **Windschutzscheibe**, -n	windscreen

fahren to drive; **abfahren** to leave, set off
einsteigen to get in; **aussteigen** to get out
sich anschnallen to put on one's seat belt
(voll)tanken to fill up (with petrol)
reisen to travel
hinten in the back; **vorn(e)** in the front

USEFUL WORDS (m)

der Abschleppwagen	breakdown van
der Anhänger ◇	trailer
der Anlasser	starter
der Ersatzreifen	spare tyre
der Fußgängerüberweg, -e	pedestrian crossing
der Kreisverkehr, -e	roundabout
der Leerlauf	neutral (gear)
der Mittelstreifen	central reservation
der Richtungsanzeiger	indicator
der Scheibenwischer	windscreen wiper
der Strafzettel	(parking) ticket
der Tachometer	speedometer
der Verkehrsrowdy, -s/-ies	road hog
der Wagenheber	jack

USEFUL WORDS (nt)

das Armaturenbrett ◇	dashboard
das Ersatzteil, -e	spare part
das Getriebe(gehäuse)	gearbox
das Kat-Auto, -s	car with a catalytic converter
das polizeiliche Kennzeichen	registration number
das Lenkrad, ̈-er	steering wheel
das Nummernschild, -er	number plate
das Steuerrad, ̈-er	steering wheel
das Todesopfer	fatality
das Verdeck, -e	hood
das Verkehrsdelikt, e	traffic offence
das Warndreieck, -e	warning triangle

gute Reise! have a good trip!
bremsen to brake; **schalten** to change gear
hupen to sound *or* toot the horn
überholen to overtake; **sich einordnen** to get into lane
abbiegen to turn off; **halten** to stop
abstellen to park; to switch off
parken to park; **ankommen** to arrive

USEFUL WORDS (f)

die Abzweigung, -en	junction
die Auffahrt, -en	slip road
die Autovermietung	car hire
die Beleuchtung	lights (pl)
die Biegung, -en	bend, curve
die Gasse, -n	alley, lane, back street
die Geschwindigkeits-begrenzung	speed limit, speed restriction
die Hupe, -n	horn, hooter
die Karosserie	bodywork, body
die Kupplung, -en	clutch
die Marke, -n	make (of car)
die (Motor)haube, -n	bonnet
die Politesse, -n	(female) traffic warden
die Starterklappe, -n	choke
die Stoßstange, -n	bumper
die (Versicherungs)police, -n	insurance policy

schnell fast; **langsam** slowly
gefährlich dangerous; **kaputt** broken, done
sperren to block; **prüfen** to check
in ein Auto fahren to bump into a car
das Auto reparieren lassen to have the car repaired
100 Kilometer in der Stunde machen to do 100 kilometres an hour
beschleunigen, Gas geben to accelerate
die Ampel überfahren to go through the lights at red
mir ist das Benzin ausgegangen I've run out of petrol
bleifrei unleaded
sich verlaufen, sich verfahren to get lost, take the wrong road
sich zurechtfinden to find one's way
trampen, per Anhalter fahren to hitch-hike
"Anlieger frei" "residents only"
"Parken verboten" "no parking"
"freihalten" "keep clear"
"achten" "give way"

ESSENTIAL WORDS (m)

der Anorak, -s	anorak
der Badeanzug, ⸚e	swimming *or* bathing costume
der Gürtel	belt
der Handschuh, -e	glove
der Kleiderschrank, ⸚e	wardrobe
der Knopf, ⸚e	button
der Mantel ⸚e	coat, overcoat
der Pullover, -s; der Pulli, -s	pullover, jumper, jersey
der Pyjama, -s	(pair of) pyjamas
der Regenmantel, ⸚	raincoat
der Rock, ⸚	skirt
der Schlips, -e	tie
der Schuh, -e	shoe
der (Spazier)stock, -e	walking stick
der Umkleideraum, (-räume)	changing room

ich ziehe mich an I get dressed, I put on my clothes
ich ziehe mich aus I get undressed, I take off my clothes
ich ziehe mich um I get changed, I change my clothes
tragen to wear
Hosen/einen Mantel tragen to wear trousers/a coat
seine Schuhe/seinen Mantel anziehen to put on one's shoes/coat
seine Schuhe/seinen Mantel ausziehen to take off one's shoes/coat
einen Hut tragen to wear a hat
sich (*dat*) **den Hut aufsetzen** to put on one's hat
den Hut abnehmen to take off one's hat
darf ich dieses Kleid anprobieren? may I try on this dress?
das steht Ihnen (gut) that suits you
passen zu fit; groß big; **klein** small
das paßt mir nicht that doesn't suit me
passend matching
waschen to wash; **bügeln** to iron
chemisch reinigen to dryclean
"vor Nässe bewahren *or* **schützen"** "keep dry"

ESSENTIAL WORDS (f)

die Badehose, -n	swimming *or* bathing trunks
die Bluse, -n	blouse
die Brille, -n	(pair of) glasses
die Größe ⌦, -n	size
die Handtasche, -n	handbag
die Hose, -n	(pair of) trousers
die Jacke, -n	jacket
die Kleidung	clothing
die Krawatte, -n	tie
die Lederhose, -n	(pair of) leather shorts
die Mode, -n	fashion
die Sandale, -n	sandal
die Socke, -n	sock
die Tasche ⌦, -n	pocket; bag

ESSENTIAL WORDS (nt)

das Abendkleid, -er	evening dress (*woman's*)
das Band ⌦, -er	ribbon
das Hemd, -en	shirt
die Jeans (*pl*)	jeans
das Kleid, -er	dress
die Kleider (*pl*)	clothes, clothing
das Nachthemd, -en	nightdress; nightshirt
das Taschentuch, -er	handkerchief
das T-Shirt, -s	T-shirt, tee-shirt

---

bunt coloured; **kariert** checked; **gestreift** striped
in Mode in fashion
modisch fashionable; **unmodisch** out of fashion
altmodisch old-fashioned
sehr schick very smart
Brustumfang (*m*) bust *or* chest measurement
Hüftweite (*f*) hip measurement
Kragenweite (*f*) collar size
Schuhgröße (*f*) shoe size
Taillenweite (*f*) waist measurement
Vorfahrt

IMPORTANT WORDS (m)

der Anzug, ̈-e	suit
der BH (Büstenhalter)	bra
der Hausschuh, -e	slipper
der Hut, ̈-e	hat
der Overall, -s	(set of) overalls
der Regenschirm, -e	umbrella
der Schal, -e *or* -s	scarf
der Schlafanzug, ̈-e	(pair of) pyjamas
der Stiefel	boot
der Strumpf, ̈-e	stocking, (long) sock
der Trainingsanzug, ̈-e	tracksuit
die Turnschuhe (*pl*)	trainers, training shoes
der Unterrock, ̈-e	underskirt, petticoat

IMPORTANT WORDS (f)

die Fliege ◇, -n	bow tie
die Freizeitkleidung	casual clothes
die Herrenkonfektion ▢	menswear
die Mode(n)schau, -en	fashion show
die Mütze, -n	cap
die Schultertasche, -n	shoulder bag
die Strumpfhose, -n	(pair of) tights
die Uniform, -en	uniform
die Unterhose, -n	(under)pants (*pl*)
die Unterwäsche	underwear
die Wäsche, -n	washing; (under)clothes

IMPORTANT WORDS (nt)

die Bermudashorts (*pl*)	Bermuda shorts
das Blouson, -e	bomber jacket
das Jackett, -s *or* -e	jacket
das Kostüm ◇, -e	costume; (lady's) suit
die Shorts (*pl*)	shorts
das Sweatshirt, -s	sweatshirt
das Unterhemd, -en	vest

USEFUL WORDS (*m*)

der Ärmel	sleeve
der Gesellschaftsanzug	evening dress (*man's*)
der Hosenanzug, ⁻e	trouser suit
der Hosenrock, ⁻e	culottes
der Hosenträger	braces (*pl*)
der Kragen	collar
die Lumpen (*pl*)	rags
der Morgenrock, ⁻e	dressing gown
der Pfennigabsatz, ⁻e	stiletto heel
der Reißverschluß, ⁻sse	zip
der Rollkragen	polo neck
der Schnürsenkel	shoelace
der Smoking, -s	dinner jacket

USEFUL WORDS (*f*)

die Falte ◇, -n	pleat
die Kappe, -n	cap, hood
die Kragenweite, -n	collar size
die Latzhose, -n	dungarees
die Melone ◇, -n	bowler hat
die Schürze, -n	apron
die Strickjacke, -n	cardigan
die Taille, -n	waist
die Tracht, -en	costume, dress
die Weste, -n	waistcoat
die Wolljacke, -n	cardigan

USEFUL WORDS (*nt*)

das Hochzeitskleid, -er	wedding dress
das Kopftuch, ⁻er	headscarf, headsquare
das Zubehör	accessories (*pl*)

sich verkleiden to disguise oneself
maskiert masked
maßgeschneidert made to measure
von der Stange off the peg

beige	beige, fawn
blau	blue
braun	brown
gelb	yellow
golden	golden
grau	grey
grün	green
orange	orange
rehbraun	fawn
rosa	pink
rot	red
schwarz	black
silbern	silver
veilchenblau	violet
violett	violet, purple
weiß	white
dunkelblau	dark blue
hellblau	light blue, pale blue
bläulich	bluish
himmelblau	sky blue
königsblau	royal blue
marineblau	navy blue

das Blau steht ihr blue suits her
etwas blau anstreichen to paint something blue

die Farbe wechseln to change colour
bunte/düstere Farben bright/dark colours
das Farbfernsehen colour television

COMPUTERS

ESSENTIAL + IMPORTANT WORDS (m)

der Buchstabe, -n	letter (of)
der Computer	computer
der Hacker	hacker
der Heimcomputer	home computer
der Joystick	joystick
der Monitor	monitor
der Personalcomputer	PC, personal computer
der Programmierer	(computer) programmer
der Rechner	computer; calculator

ESSENTIAL + IMPORTANT WORDS (f)

die Batterie, -n	battery
die Computerlehre	computer studies
die Funktion, -en	function
die Hardware	hardware
die Software	software
die Taste ◇, -n ▢	key

ESSENTIAL + IMPORTANT WORDS (nt)

die Daten (pl)	data
das Kilobyte	kilobyte
das Megabyte	megabyte
das Menü, -s	menu
das Programm ◇, -e	program
das Programmieren	(computer) programming
das RAM	RAM (random access memory)
ROM	ROM (read only memory)

...s it?

people, leaves)

...as a berry

die ... green card (*for motor*

die Grün...

Rotkäppchen ... Riding Hood

in den roten Za... ...the red, in debt

in den schwarzen ...llen in the black

ein Schwarzer a black man

eine Schwarze a black woman

ein Schwarzes Brett a notice board

ein Weißer a white man

eine Weiße a white woman

das Weiße Haus the White House

schneeweiß as white as snow

leichenblaß as white as a sheet

50

USEFUL WORDS (m)

der Ausdruck ⟲, ⸚e	print-out
der Bildschirm, -e	monitor, screen
der Cursor	cursor
der Drucker	printer
der Laserdrucker	laser printer
der Speicher	memory

USEFUL WORDS (f)

die Datei	file
die Datenbank	data base
die Diskette, -n	disk; floppy disk
die Festplatte, -n	hard disk
die Informatik	computer science, computing
die Maus, Mäuse	mouse
die Schnittstelle, -n	interface
die Sicherungskopie, -n	back-up (copy)
die Tastatur	keyboard

USEFUL WORDS (nt)

das Bildschirmgerät, -e or **Datensichtgerät, -e**	VDU, visual display unit
das Computerspiel	computer game
das Diskettenlaufwerk	disk drive
das Interface	interface
das Modem	modem
das Textverarbeitungsgerät, -e	word processor

die Daten speichern to store the data
die Daten sicherstellen to save the data
eine Auskunft wiederbekommen to retrieve a piece of information
ausdrucken to print out
tragbar portable

COUNTRIES

All countries are neuter unless marked otherwise. Where an article is shown, the noun is used with the article.

Afrika	Africa
Asien	Asia
Australien	Australia
Belgien	Belgium
Brasilien	Brazil
Bulgarien	Bulgaria
die **Bundesrepublik Deutschland (BRD)**	West Germany
China	China
Dänemark	Denmark
die **DDR (Deutsche Demokratische Republik)**	East Germany
Deutschland	Germany
England	England
Europa	Europe
die **europäische (Wirtschafts) gemeinschaft (E(W)G)**	the European (Economic) Community, (E(E)C)
Finnland	Finland
Frankreich	France
der **Gemeinsame Markt**	the Common Market
Großbritannien	Great Britain
Griechenland	Greece
Holland	Holland
Indien	India
der **Irak**	Iraq
der **Iran**	Iran
Irland	Ireland
Italien	Italy
Japan	Japan
Jugoslawien	Yugoslavia
Kanada	Canada
Korea	Korea
Kuwait	Kuwait

COUNTRIES (cont)

der **Libanon**	Lebanon
Luxemburg	Luxemburg
Marokko	Morocco
Mexiko	Mexico
Neuseeland	New Zealand
die **Niederlande** (pl)	the Netherlands
Nordirland	Northern Ireland
Norwegen	Norway
Österreich	Austria
Pakistan	Pakistan
Polen	Poland
Portugal	Portugal
Rumänien	Romania
Rußland	Russia
Saudi-Arabien	Saudi Arabia
Schottland	Scotland
Schweden	Sweden
die **Schweiz**	Switzerland
Skandinavien	Scandinavia
die **Sowjetunion**	the Soviet Union, Russia
Spanien	Spain
Südafrika	South Africa
Südamerika	South America
die **Tschechoslowakei**	Czechoslovakia
die **Türkei**	Turkey
die **UdSSR**	USSR, Russia
Ungarn	Hungary
das **Vereinigte Königreich**	the United Kingdom
die **Vereinigten Staaten**	the United States
(mpl) **(von Amerika)**	(of America)
Vietnam	Vietnam
Wales	Wales

in die Niederlande/in die Sowjetunion fahren to go to the
   Netherlands/to the Soviet Union
nach Deutschland fahren to go to Germany

COUNTRIES (cont)

ein Land, (pl) **Länder** country
die Entwicklungsländer (pl) developing countries
ins Ausland fahren or **gehen** to go or travel abroad
im Ausland sein to be abroad
von Übersee from overseas
ein Ausländer, eine Ausländerin a foreigner
ein Fremder, eine Fremde a stranger
ausländisch foreign
fremd strange, foreign
die Hauptstadt capital
ich bin in Deutschland geboren I was born in Germany

NATIONALITIES (m)

ein Afrikaner	an African
ein Amerikaner	an American
ein Araber	an Arab
ein Asiat	an Asian
ein Australier	an Australian
ein Belgier	a Belgian
ein Brasilianer	a Brazilian
ein Brite	a Briton (pl the British)
ein Bulgare	a Bulgar, a Bulgarian
ein Chinese	a Chinese
ein Däne	a Dane
Deutsche(r)	a German
ein Engländer	an Englishman
ein Europäer	a European
ein Finne	a Finn
ein Franzose	a Frenchman
ein Grieche	a Greek
ein Holländer	a Dutchman

NATIONALITIES (m) (cont)

ein **Inder**	an Indian
ein **Iraker**	an Iraqi
ein **Iraner**	an Iranian
ein **Japaner**	a Japanese
ein **Jugoslawe**	a Yugoslav
ein **Kanadier**	a Canadian
ein **Kuwaiter**	a Kuwaiti
ein **Libanese**	a Lebanese
ein **Luxemburger**	a native of Luxemburg
ein **Mexikaner**	a Mexican
ein **Neuseeländer**	a New Zealander
ein **Norweger**	a Norwegian
ein **Österreicher**	an Austrian
ein **Pakistaner**	a Pakistani
ein **Pole**	a Pole
ein **Portugiese**	a Portuguese
ein **Rumäne**	a Romanian
ein **Russe**	a Russian
ein **Schotte**	a Scotsman, a Scot
ein **Schwede**	a Swede
ein **Schweizer**	a Swiss
ein **Sowjetbürger**	a Soviet citizen
ein **Spanier**	a Spaniard
ein **Tschechoslowake**	a Czech, a Czechoslovakian
ein **Türke**	a Turk
ein **Ungar**	a Hungarian
ein **Vietnamese**	a Vietnamese
ein **Waliser**	a Welshman

The forms given above and on the following two pages are the
noun forms. The corresponding adjectives begin with a small
letter and end in **-isch**.
Most can be formed by changing **-er(in)** or **-ier(in)** to **-isch**.
The main exceptions are as follows: **deutsch** (*German*),
englisch (*English*), **französisch** (*French*), **schweizerisch**
(*Swiss*), **sowjetisch** (*Russian*).

NATIONALITIES (f)	
eine **Afrikanerin**	an African (girl *or* woman)
eine **Amerikanerin**	an American (girl *or* woman)
eine **Araberin**	an Arabian (girl *or* woman)
eine **Asiatin**	an Asian (girl *or* woman)
eine **Australierin**	an Australian (girl *or* woman)
eine **Belgierin**	a Belgian (girl *or* woman)
eine **Brasilianerin**	a Brazilian (girl *or* woman)
eine **Britin**	a Briton, a British girl *or* woman
eine **Bulgarin**	a Bulgarian (girl *or* woman)
eine **Chinesin**	a Chinese (girl *or* woman)
eine **Dänin**	a Dane, a Danish girl *or* woman
eine **Deutsche**	a German (girl *or* woman)
eine **Engländerin**	an Englishwoman, an English girl
eine **Europäerin**	a European (girl *or* woman)
eine **Finnin**	a Finn, a Finnish girl *or* woman
eine **Französin**	a Frenchwoman, a French girl
eine **Griechin**	a Greek, a Greek girl *or* woman
eine **Holländerin**	a Dutchwoman, a Dutch girl
eine **Inderin**	an Indian (girl *or* woman)
eine **Irakerin**	an Iraqi (girl *or* woman)
eine **Iranerin**	an Iranian (girl *or* woman)
eine **Irin**	an Irishwoman, an Irish girl
eine **Italienerin**	an Italian (girl *or* woman)
eine **Japanerin**	a Japanese (girl *or* woman)
eine **Jugoslawin**	a Yugoslav, a Yugoslavian girl *or* woman
eine **Kanadierin**	a Canadian (girl *or* woman)
eine **Kuwaiterin**	a Kuwaiti (girl *or* woman)
eine **Libanesin**	a Lebanese (girl *or* woman)
eine **Luxemburgerin**	a native of Luxemburg
eine **Mexikanerin**	a Mexican (girl *or* woman)
eine **Neuseeländerin**	a New Zealander, a New Zealand girl *or* woman
eine **Norwegerin**	a Norwegian (girl *or* woman)
eine **Österreicherin**	an Austrian (girl *or* woman)
eine **Pakistanerin**	a Pakistani (girl *or* woman)

NATIONALITIES (f) (cont)

eine Polin	a Pole, a Polish girl *or* woman
eine Portugiesin	a Portuguese (girl *or* woman)
eine Rumänin	a Rumanian (girl *or* woman)
eine Russin	a Russian (girl *or* woman)
eine Schottin	a Scotswoman, a Scots girl
eine Schwedin	a Swede, a Swedish girl *or* woman
eine Schweizerin	a Swiss girl *or* woman
eine Sowjetbürgerin	a Soviet citizen
eine Spanierin	a Spaniard, a Spanish girl *or* woman
eine Tschechoslowakin	a Czech, a Czechoslovakian (girl *or* woman)
eine Türkin	a Turkish girl *or* woman
eine Ungarin	a Hungarian (girl *or* woman)
eine Vietnamesin	a Vietnamese (girl *or* woman)
eine Waliserin	a Welshwoman, a Welsh girl

die Staatsangehörigkeit nationality	
die Religion religion	
die Heimat native country	
die Muttersprache native language	
christlich Christian	
evangelisch Protestant	
jüdisch Jewish	
katholisch Catholic	
moslemisch Moslem, Muslim	

ESSENTIAL WORDS (m)

der Bauernhof, ⸚e	farmyard, farm
der Baum, Bäume	tree
der Berg ⬦, -e	mountain, hill
der Fluß, ⸚sse	river
der Gasthof, ⸚e	inn
der Grund ⬦	ground
der Hügel	hill
der Lärm	noise
der Markt, ⸚e	market
der See ⬦, -n	lake
der Stein, -e	stone, rock
der Stock, ⸚e	cane, stick
der Turm, ⸚e	tower; (church) steeple
der Wald, ⸚er	wood, forest

ESSENTIAL WORDS (nt)

das Dorf, ⸚er	village
das Feld, -er	field
das Gasthaus, (-häuser)	inn
das Land ⬦, ⸚er	land, country
das Picknick, -e *or* -s	picnic
das Schloß ⬦, ⸚sser	castle
das Tal, ⸚er	valley
das Wirtshaus, (-haüser)	inn

aufs Land gehen to go into the country
auf dem Lande wohnen to live in the country
auf dem Bauernhof on the farm
ein Picknick machen to go for a picnic
im Freien in the open air

ESSENTIAL WORDS (f)

die Blume, -n	flower
die Brücke ⇨, -n	bridge
die Burg, -en	castle
die Höhle, -n	cave, hole
die Jugendherberge, -n	youth hostel
die Kirche, -n	church
die Landschaft	countryside, scenery
die Landstraße, -n	country road
die Luft	air
die Straße, -n	road, street
die Wiese, -n	meadow

hügelig hilly; **flach** flat; **steil** steep
ruhig peaceful
fruchtbar fertile; **schlecht** bad, poor
kultivieren, anbauen to cultivate, grow
fließen to flow
bummeln to wander, stroll
überqueren to cross
jagen to hunt; to shoot
in einer Jugendherberge übernachten to spend the night in
   a youth hostel
sich auf den Weg machen to set out, set off
der Weg zum Dorf the way to the village
in der Ferne in the distance

IMPORTANT WORDS (m)

der Bach, ⸚e 📖	stream, brook
der Bauer, -n 📖	farmer; peasant; (pl) countryfolk
der Boden ◇	ground, earth
der Forst, -e 📖	forest
der Friede(n)	peace
der Gipfel 📖	(mountain) top
der Gummistiefel	wellington (boot)
der Spazierstock, ⸚e	walking stick
der Stiefel	boot
der Strom ◇, ⸚e	river
der Tourist, -en	tourist
der Wasserfall, ⸚e	waterfall
der Weg ◇, -e	path, way, road

IMPORTANT WORDS (f)

die Bäuerin 📖	lady farmer; farmer's wife; peasant
die Bauersfrau, -en	farmer's wife
die Erde, -n	earth, soil
die Gegend, -en	district, area
die Heide ◇, -n	heath; heather
die Landwirtschaft	agriculture, farming
die Talsperre, -n 📖	dam

IMPORTANT WORDS (nt)

das Bauernhaus, (-häuser)	farmhouse
das Fernglas, ⸚er	(pair of) binoculars
das Flachland, ⸚er	lowlands (pl)
das Gebiet, -e 📖	area
das Gebirge 📖	mountain chain
das Heideland	heath
das Heu	hay
das Korn	corn, grain
das Tor ◇, -e	gate
das Ufer ◇ 📖	(river) bank

USEFUL WORDS (m)

der Acker, ⸚	field
der Bewohner	inhabitant
der Dorfbewohner	villager
der Erdboden, ⸚	ground
der Jäger	hunter
der Landwirt, -e	farmer
der Pfad, -e	path
der Schlamm	mud
der Sumpf, ⸚e	marsh
der Teich, -e	pond
der Wegweiser	signpost
der Weiher	pond, lake
der Weiler	hamlet
der Weinberg, -e	vineyard
der Wipfel	treetop

USEFUL WORDS (f)

die Ebene, -n	plain
die Ernte, -n	harvest, crop
die Falle, -n	trap
die Gemeinde, -n	community
die Hecke, -n	hedge
die Jagd, -en	hunt; hunting
die Quelle, -n	spring; source
die Spitze ◇, -n	tip, peak, point
die (Wind)mühle, -n	(wind)mill

USEFUL WORDS (nt)

das Geräusch, -e	noise, sound
das Getreide	grain, cereal crop
das Grundstück, -e	estate; plot of land
das Heidekraut	heather
das Loch, ⸚er	hole

ESSENTIAL WORDS (m)

der Bart, ⸚e	beard
der Herr, -en	gentleman
der Junge, -n	boy
der Mann ◇, ⸚er	man
der Mensch, -en	human being; man; person
der (Personal)ausweis, -e	identity card
der Schnurrbart, ⸚e	moustache

ESSENTIAL WORDS (f)

die Ähnlichkeit, -en (mit) 📖	similarity (to)
die Bewegung, -en 📖	movement, motion
die Brille, -n	(pair of) glasses
die Dame, -n	lady
die Frau ◇, -en	woman
die Gesichtsfarbe, -n	complexion
die Größe ◇, -n	height; size
die Person, -en	person
die Schönheit	beauty

ESSENTIAL WORDS (nt)

das Alter ◇ 📖	age
das Auge, -n	eye
das Aussehen	appearance
das Fräulein	young lady
das Haar, -e	hair
das Mädchen	girl

ich heiße Wolfgang my name is Wolfgang
wie heißen Sie? what is your name?
jung young; **alt** old
wie alt sind Sie? how old are you?, what age are you?
ich bin 16 Jahre alt I am 16 (years old)
mittleren Alters middle-aged

bärtig bearded; **schnurrbärtig** with a moustache
glatt rasiert clean-shaven
er sieht wie sein Vater aus/wie seine Mutter aus he looks
   like his father/his mother
er ist seinem Vater/seiner Mutter ähnlich he resembles his
   father/his mother
erkennen to recognize
müde/zornig/komisch aussehen to look tired/angry/funny
ein gutaussehender Mann a handsome *or* good-looking man
eine schöne Dame a beautiful lady
groß tall, big; **klein** short, small; **lang** long; **kurz** short
ein Mann von mittlerer Größe a man of medium height
sie ist 1 Meter 70 groß she is 1 metre 70 tall
grüne/blaue/braune Augen haben to have green/blue/
   brown eyes
Kontaktlinsen/eine Brille tragen to wear contact lenses/
   glasses
er hat blonde/dunkle/schwarze/rote/graue Haare he has
   blond *or* fair/dark/black/red/grey hair
rothaarig red-haired
eine Glatze bekommen to be going bald
lockiges/welliges/glattes Haar curly/wavy/straight hair
ihre neue Frisur steht ihr gut her new hairstyle suits her
sich benehmen to behave (oneself)
weinen to cry; **lachen** to laugh; **lächeln** to smile
vor Freude lachen/weinen to laugh/cry with joy
eine gute Figur haben to have a nice figure
von schlanker/schwerer Gestalt sein to be of slender/heavy
   build
wieviel wiegst du? what do you weigh?
die Gewohnheit haben, etw zu tun to have a habit of doing
   sth
(nicht) in der Laune *or* **in der Stimmung für etw sein** (not)
   to be in the mood for sth
gut/schlecht gelaunt in a good/bad mood
auf jdn böse sein to be angry with sb
ärgern to annoy

IMPORTANT WORDS (m)

der Charakter	character
der Gang ◇, ⁼e 🕮	walk, gait
der Mangel, ⁼	defect, fault
der Zorn	anger

IMPORTANT WORDS (f)

die Figur ◇, -en	figure
die Freude	joy, delight
die Geste, -n	gesture
die Kontaktlinsen (pl)	contact lenses
die Natur, -en	nature
die Neugierigkeit 🕮	curiosity
die Schüchternheit	shyness

IMPORTANT WORDS (nt)

das Gewicht, -e	weight
das Wesen	character, personality

USEFUL WORDS (m)

der Ausdruck ◇, ⁼e	expression
der Faulenzer	lazybones
der Gesichtszug, ⁼e	(facial) feature
der Körperbau	build
der Leberfleck, -e	mole
der Pickel ◇	spot, pimple
der Pony ◇, -s	fringe
der Riese, -n	giant
der Schönheitsfleck, -e	beauty spot
der Schweiß	sweat, perspiration
der Taugenichts	good-for-nothing
der Teint, -s	complexion
der Zug ◇, ⁼e	feature

USEFUL WORDS (f)

die **Ängstlichkeit**	nervousness
die **Dauerwelle, -n**	perm
die **Eigenschaft, -en**	quality, attribute
die **Falte** ⟳, **-n**	wrinkle
die **Faulenzerin**	lazybones
die **Frisur, -en**	hairstyle
die **Gestalt, -en**	figure
die **Gewohnheit, -en**	habit
die **Glatze, -n**	bald head
die **Häßlichkeit**	ugliness
die **Laune, -n**	mood, humour, temper
die **Locke, -n**	curl
die **Narbe, -n**	scar
die **Runzel, -n**	wrinkle
die **Schlafmütze, -n**	sleepyhead
die **Sommersprosse, -n**	freckle
die **Stimmung, -en**	mood, frame of mind
die **Träne, -n**	tear
die **Wut**	fury, rage

USEFUL WORDS (nt)

das **Benehmen**	behaviour
das **Doppelkinn, -e**	double chin
das **Gebiß, -sse**	false teeth
das **Gefühl, -e**	feeling
das **Gewissen**	conscience
das **Grübchen**	dimple
das **(Lebe)wesen**	creature
das **Selbstvertrauen**	self-confidence

ähnlich (+ *dat*)	similar (to), like
ängstlich	nervous, worried
auffallend	striking
blaß	pale
blind	blind
böse	angry; evil
bucklig	hunch-backed
dick	fat
dumm	stupid
dünn	thin
Durchschnitts-	average
ehrlich	honest
eifersüchtig (auf + *acc*)	jealous (of)
einsam	lonely
enttäuscht	disappointed
ernst	serious
frech (zu + *dat*)	cheeky (to)
freundlich (zu + *dat*)	friendly (to), kind (to)
froh, fröhlich	glad, happy
gebräunt	tanned
geduldig	patient
geschickt	skilful, clever
glücklich	happy
grausam	cruel
groß	tall; big
gutmütig	good-natured
häßlich	ugly
hell	fair (*skin*); light
homosexuell	homosexual
hübsch	pretty
intelligent	intelligent
klein	small
klug	clever
komisch	funny
kräftig	strong
kurz	short
kurzsichtig/weitsichtig	short-sighted/long-sighted

ESSENTIAL WORDS (f)

die **Abschlußprüfung**	final exam
die **Antwort, -en**	answer
die **Arbeit** ⟁, **-en**	work; test
die **Arithmetik**	arithmetic
die **Aufgabe, -n**	exercise, task
die **Bibliothek, -en**	library
die **Biologie**	biology
die **Chemie**	chemistry
die **Computerlehre**	computer studies
die **Direktorin**	headmistress (*of secondary school*)
die **Erdkunde**	geography
die **Frage, -n**	question
die **Freundin**	friend
die **Geographie**	geography
die **Gesamtschule, -n**	comprehensive school
die **Geschichte, -n**	history; story
die **Grundschule, -n**	primary school
die **Gruppe, -n**	group
die **Handarbeit**	handicrafts; needlework
die **Hauptschule, -n** ▢	secondary school
die **Hausaufgabe, -n**	homework
die **Holzarbeiten** (*pl*)	woodwork
die **Karte,** ⟁, **-n**	map; card
die **Klasse, -n**	class, form
die **Klassenarbeit, -en** ▢	test
die **Klassenfahrt, -en** ▢	(class) trip, outing
die **Klassenlehrerin**	form teacher
die **Kreide**	chalk
die **Kunst**	art
die **Lehrerin**	(school)teacher
die **Mappe, -n**	briefcase; folder
die **Mathematik; die Mathe**	mathematics, maths
die **Mittagspause, -n**	lunch break
die **Musik**	music
die **Pause** ⟁, **-n**	break, interval
die **Physik**	physics

die Schule besuchen to attend school
in der Schule at school
ich gehe in die Schule I'm going to school
arbeiten to work
aufpassen to pay attention; **zuhören** to listen
lernen to learn; **studieren** to study; **vergessen** to forget
lesen to read; **schreiben** to write; **sprechen** to speak
sprichst du Deutsch? do you speak German?
seit wieviele Jahren lernen Sie Deutsch? how many years have you been learning German?
ich lerne Deutsch seit 3 Jahren I've been learning German for 3 years
lehren, unterrichten to teach
ich möchte Lehrer werden I'd like to be a teacher
der Französischlehrer the French teacher (*teacher of French*)
eine Prüfung machen to sit an exam
das Abitur machen to sit one's A-levels (*approx*)
wiederholen to repeat; to revise
mündlich oral; **schriftlich** written
eine Prüfung bestehen/nicht bestehen to pass/fail an exam
den ersten Preis gewinnen to win first prize
durchfallen to fail
sitzenbleiben to repeat a year
Fortschritte machen to make progress
versetzen to move *or* put up
die Schule verlassen to leave school
klug clever; **intelligent** intelligent; **dumm** stupid
fragen to ask; **antworten** to answer, reply
jdm eine Frage stellen to ask sb a question
eine Frage beantworten to answer a question

ESSENTIAL WORDS (f) (cont)

die Prüfung, -en	exam, examination
die Realschule, -n □	secondary school
die (höhere) Schule *or*	(secondary) school
die Schülerin	schoolgirl, pupil; student
die Schulfreundin *or*	
die Schulkameradin	schoolfriend
die Schultasche, -n	satchel, school bag
die Seite ◇, -n	page
die Sozialkunde	modern studies
die Stunde ◇, -n	lesson, period
die Tafel ◇, -n	blackboard
die Technik	technology
die Tinte	ink
die Turnhalle, -n	gym, gymnasium
die Universität, -en; die Uni	university

ESSENTIAL WORDS (nt)

das Buch, ̈er	book
das Deutsch	German
das Englisch	English
das Examen, - *or* Examina	exam, examination
das Französisch	French
das Gymnasium, -ien	grammar school
das Klassenzimmer	classroom, schoolroom
das Lineal, -e	ruler
das Papier, -e	paper
das (Schul)fach, ̈er	(school) subject
das (Schul)heft, -e	exercise book
das Semester	term (*2 per year*)
das Spanisch	Spanish
Technisches Zeichnen	technical drawing
das Trimester	term (*3 per year*)
das Turnen ◇	P.E.; gymnastics
das Werken	handicrafts
das Wörterbuch, ̈er	dictionary

IMPORTANT WORDS (m)	
der Austausch, -e	exchange
der Buchstabe, -n	letter of alphabet
der Erfolg, -e ▱	success
der Fehler	mistake, error; fault
der Feiertag, -e	holiday, day off
der Gummi, -s	rubber
der Hochschüler	college student
der Klassensprecher ▱	form prefect
der Kursus, Kurse	course
der Mitschüler	classmate, schoolmate
der Rektor	headmaster (*primary*); rector
der Schlafsaal, (-säle)	dormitory
der Schülerlotse, -n ▱	*pupil who helps with school crossing patrol*
der Student, -en	student
der Zettel	piece of paper; note; form

IMPORTANT WORDS (nt)	
das Abitur	German school-leaving certificate/exam
das Bestehen	pass (*in exam*)
das Blatt ◇, ̈-er	sheet (*of paper*); newspaper
das Diplom, -e	diploma
das Ergebnis, -se ▱	result (*of exam*)
das Italienisch	Italian
das Latein	Latin
das Lehrerzimmer	staff room
das Pflichtfach, ̈-er	compulsory subject
das Rechnen	arithmetic
das (Schul)zeugnis, -se	(school) report
das (Sprach)labor	(language) lab
das Vokabular	vocabulary
das Wahlfach, ̈-er	option, optional subject
das Zeichnen	drawing (*subject*)

IMPORTANT WORDS (f)

die Algebra	algebra
die Aula, Aulen *or* -s	assembly hall
die Berufsschule, -n □	vocational *or* trade school
die Fach(hoch)schule, -n	technical college
die Fremdsprache, -n	foreign language
die Ganztagsschule	all-day school *or* schooling
die Garderobe ◇, -n	cloakroom
die Geometrie	geometry
die Grammatik	grammar
die Halbtagsschule □	half-day school
die Hochschule, -n	college; university
die technische Hochschule, -n -n	technical college
die Koedukationsschule, -n	mixed school, co-ed
die Lehre	teaching
die Leistung, -en □	achievement
die Methode, -n	method
die Mitschülerin	classmate, schoolmate
die Nachhilfe □	private coaching *or* tuition
die Näherei	sewing, needlework
die Naturwissenschaft □	natural history
die Note ◇, -n	mark, grade
die Oberstufe	upper school
die Reihe ◇, -n	row (*of seats etc*)
die Rektorin	headmistress (*primary*)
die Religion	religion
die gemischte Schule	mixed school, co-ed
die Schülermitverwaltung (SMV) □	school *or* student council
die Sprache, -n	language
die neueren Sprachen	modern languages
die Strafarbeit, -en	punishment exercise
die Studentin	student
die Übersetzung, -en	translation
die Übung, -en	practice; exercise
die Zeichnung, -en	drawing (*piece of work*)

USEFUL WORDS (m)

die Abwesenden (pl)	absentees
die Anwesenden (pl)	those present
der Aufsatz, ⸚	composition, essay
der Aufsichtsschüler	prefect
der Bericht, -e	report
der Bleistiftspitzer	pencil sharpener
der Drehbleistift, -e	propelling pencil
der Federhalter	(fountain) pen
die Fortschritte (pl)	progress
der Füllfederhalter; der Füller	fountain pen
der Gang ⌂, ⸚e	corridor
der Gesang	singing
der Internatsschüler	boarder
der Irrtum, ⸚er	error
der Klecks, -e	blot, stain
der Religionsunterricht	religious education
der Satz ⌂, ⸚e	sentence
der Tagesschüler	day-boy
der Vortrag, ⸚e	talk, lecture

---

schwierig difficult; **einfach** easy
interessant interesting; **langweilig** boring
faul lazy; **fleißig** hard-working; **streng** strict
mein Lieblingsfach my favourite subject
letztes Jahr habe ich einen Austausch gemacht I did an exchange last year
schulfrei haben to have a day off
hitzefrei haben to have a day off because of very hot weather

---

USEFUL WORDS (f)

die Aktentasche, -n	briefcase
die Aufsichtsschülerin	prefect
die Dichtung	poetry
die Erziehung	education, schooling
die Handelshochschule, -n	commercial college
die Hauswirtschaft	home economics
die Internatsschülerin	boarder
die Kantine, -n	canteen
die Lektion, -en	lesson, unit
die Lektüre	reading
die Pädagogische Hochschule (P.H.)	College of Education
die Preisverleihung, -en	prize-giving
die Rechtschreibung	spelling
die Regel, -n	rule
die Tagesschülerin	day-girl
die Volksschule, -n	primary school
die Vorlesung, -en	lecture

USEFUL WORDS (nt)

das Benehmen	behaviour, conduct
das Diktat	dictation
das Griechisch	Greek
das Internat, -e	boarding school
das Nachsitzen	detention
das Notizbuch, ⁻er	jotter; notebook
das Pult, -e	desk
das Russisch	Russian
das Studenten(wohn)heim, -e	students' hall of residence
das Tonbandgerät, -e	tape recorder

abschreiben to copy
die Schule schwänzen to skip school
bestrafen to punish; **loben** to praise
jdn nachsitzen lassen to keep sb in (after school)

ESSENTIAL WORDS (m)	
der Baum, Bäume	tree
der Berg ◊, -e	hill, mountain
der Fisch, -e	fish
der Fluß, ̈sse	river
der Regen	rain
der See ◊, -n	lake
der Strand, ̈e	beach
der Wald, ̈er	forest, wood

ESSENTIAL WORDS (f)	
die Blume, -n	flower
die Fabrik, -en	factory
die Flasche, -n	bottle
die Frage, -n	question
die Insel, -n	island
die Luft	air
die See ◊, -n	sea
die Temperatur, -en	temperature
die Welt	world
die Zeit, -en	time
die Zeitschrift, -en	magazine
die Zeitung, -en	newspaper

ESSENTIAL WORDS (nt)	
das Auto, -s	car
das Benzin	petrol
das Essen ◊	food
das Gas, -e	gas
die Gemüse (*pl*)	vegetables
das Glas, ̈er	glass
das Land ◊, ̈er	country
das Meer, -e	ocean; sea
das Obst	fruit
das Tier, -e	animal
das Wasser	water
das Wetter	weather

eine Weltreise machen to go round the world
das höchste/größte/schönste der Welt the highest/
  biggest/most beautiful in the world
ferne Länder far-off countries
im/ins Ausland (*being*) abroad/(*going*) abroad
in der Zukunft in future
verschmutzen to pollute
zerstören to destroy
verunreinigen to contaminate
etw verbieten to ban sth
retten to save
wiederaufbereiten to recycle
biologisch abbaubar biodegradable
umweltfreundlich environment-friendly
umweltschädlich harmful to the environment
grün green
organisch organic
bleifrei unleaded

IMPORTANT WORDS (m)

der Abfall	waste
der Einwohner	inhabitant
der Forst, -e 🔲	forest
die Grünen (pl)	the Greens
der Kanal, Kanäle	canal
der Mond	moon
der Planet, -en	planet
die tropischen Regenwälder (pl)	tropical rainforests
Saure(r) Regen	acid rain
der Strom ◇, ⁼e	river

IMPORTANT WORDS (f)

die Erde	the earth
die Gegend, -en	region, area
die Hitze	heat
die Katastrophe, -n	catastrophe
die Küste, -n	coast
die Lösung, -en	solution
die Pflanze, -n	plant
die Zukunft	future

IMPORTANT WORDS (nt)

das Aluminium	aluminium
das Deodorant -s or -e	deodorant
das Gebiet, -e 🔲	area
das Holz	wood
das Klima, -s or -te	climate
das Produkt, -e	product; (pl) produce
das Spülmittel	washing-up liquid
das Waschmittel	detergent
das Waschpulver	washing powder

USEFUL WORDS (m)

der Brennstoff	fuel (*for heating*)
der Dieselkraftstoff	diesel oil
die FCKW (*pl*)	CFC's
der Forscher	researcher
der Katalysator	catalytic converter
der Ökologe, -n	ecologist
der Ozean, -e	ocean
der Schaden, ̈:	damage, harm
der Treibhauseffekt	the greenhouse effect
der Treibstoff	fuel (*for vehicles*)
der Umweltschutz	conservation
der Umweltschützer	conservationist, environmentalist
der Wissenschaftler	scientist

USEFUL WORDS (f)

die Bevölkerung, -en	population
die Chemikalien (*pl*)	chemicals
die globale Erwärmung	global warming
die Krise, -n	crisis
die Ökologin	ecologist
die Ozonschicht	ozone layer
die Regierung, -en	government
die Sprühdose, -n	aerosol
die Steuer ◇, -n	tax
die Umwelt	environment
die (Umwelt)verschmutzung	(environmental) pollution
die Wüste, -n	desert

USEFUL WORDS (nt)

die Abwässer (*pl*)	sewage
das Erdbeben	earthquake
das Ereignis, -se	event
das Loch, ̈-er	hole
das Weltall	universe

ESSENTIAL WORDS (m)	
der Alte(r), -n	old man/woman
der Babysitter	babysitter
der Bruder, ¨	brother
die Eltern (pl)	parents
der Erwachsene(r)	grown-up, adult
der Familienname, -n	surname
der Freund, -e	friend
die Geschwister (pl)	brothers and sisters
der Großvater, ¨	grandfather
der Junge, -n	boy
die Leute (pl)	people
der Mädchenname, -n	maiden name
der Mann ⋄, ¨er	man; husband
der junge Mann	youth, young man
der Mensch, -en	human being, person
der Name, -n	name
der Onkel	uncle
der Opa; **der** Opi	grandpa
der Sohn, ¨e	son
der Vater, ¨	father
der Vati, -s 📖	dad, daddy
der Vorname, -n	first name, Christian name
der Zwilling, -e	twin
der Zwillingsbruder, ¨	twin brother

ich heiße Karl my name is Karl
ich bin 17 Jahre alt I am 17 (years old)
ich bin im 1974 geboren I was born in 1974
wie heißt du? — wie alt bist du? what's your name? — how old are you?
wir nennen das Baby Ludo we call the baby Ludo
männlich male; **weiblich** female
kennen to know; **kennenlernen** to get to know
vorstellen to introduce; **erinnern (an + acc)** to remind (of)
unsere Familie stammt aus Polen our family comes from Poland
wir wohnen jetzt in Österreich we live in Austria now

ESSENTIAL WORDS (f)

die Dame, -n	lady
die Familie, -n	family
die Frau ◇, **-en**	woman; wife
die Freundin	friend
die Großmutter, ⸚	grandmother
die Hausfrau, -en	housewife
die Mutter, ⸚	mother
die Mutti, -s ▭	mum, mummy
die Oma; die Omi	granny
die Person, -en	person
die Schwester, -n	sister
die Tante, -n	aunt
die Tochter, ⸚	daughter
die Zwillingsschwester, -n	twin sister

ESSENTIAL WORDS (nt)

das Alter ◇ ▭	age; old age
das Baby, -s	baby
das Einzelkind, -er	only child
das Fräulein	young lady
das Kind, -er	child
das Mädchen	(young) girl
das Paar ◇, **-e**	couple

---

verlobt engaged; **verheiratet** married
ledig single; **geschieden** divorced
meine Eltern leben getrennt my parents are separated
sich verloben to get engaged
sich verheiraten to get married
sich scheiden lassen to get divorced
älter/jünger als ich older/younger than me
die ganze Familie the whole family
bei uns at or to our place, at or to our house
mein Großvater ist im 1990 gestorben my grandfather died
  in 1990
tot dead
streiten to quarrel; **sich vertragen** to get along

IMPORTANT WORDS (m)

der Austauschpartner	partner (*in an exchange*)
Bekannte(r)	acquaintance
der Cousin, -s	cousin
der Ehemann, ⸚er	married man; husband
der Enkel ⌑	grandson; (*pl*) grandchildren
Jugendliche(r) ⌑	teenager, young person
der Nachbar, -n	neighbour
der Nachname, -n	surname
der Neffe, -n ⌑	nephew
der Rentner ⌑	(old age) pensioner
der Schwiegersohn, ⸚e	son-in-law
der Schwiegervater, ⸚	father-in-law
Verlobte(r), -n	fiancé/fiancée
Verwandte(r), -n	relation, relative
der Vetter, -n	cousin
der Witwer ⌑	widower

IMPORTANT WORDS (f)

die Cousine, -n	cousin
die Ehefrau, -en	married woman; wife
die Enkelin	granddaughter
die Jugend	youth (*stage of life*)
die Kusine, -n ⌑	cousin
die Nachbarin	neighbour
die Nichte, -n ⌑	niece
die Rentnerin ⌑	(old age) pensioner
die Schwiegermutter, ⸚	mother-in-law
die Schwiegertochter, ⸚	daughter-in-law
die Witwe, -n ⌑	widow

IMPORTANT WORDS (nt)

das Au-pair, -s	au pair
das Ehepaar, -e ⌑	married couple
das Enkelkind	grandchild
das Kindermädchen	nanny

USEFUL WORDS (m)

der Bräutigam, -e	bridegroom
die Drillinge (pl)	triplets
der Junggeselle, -n	bachelor
die Jungverheirateten (pl)	newly-weds
der Pate, -n	godfather
der Rufname, -n	first name, usual name
der Säugling, -e	baby, infant
der Schwager, ¨	brother-in-law
der Spitzname, -n	nickname
der Stiefbruder, ¨	stepbrother
der Stiefvater, ¨	stepfather
der Vorfahr, -en	ancestor
der Vormund, -e or ¨er	guardian
der Zuname, -n	surname

USEFUL WORDS (f)

die Braut, Bräute	bride
die Hochzeit, -en	wedding
die alte Jungfer, -n -n	spinster, old maid
die Junggesellin	unmarried woman
die Patin	godmother
die Schwägerin	sister-in-law
die Stiefmutter, ¨	stepmother
die Stiefschwester, -n	stepsister
die Waise, -n	orphan

USEFUL WORDS (nt)

das Greisenalter	(extreme) old age
das Waisenhaus, ¨er	orphanage
das Weib, -er	woman (old-fashioned or pejorative)

ESSENTIAL WORDS (m)

der Bauer ⇔, -n ▢	farmer; peasant, countryman
der Bauernhof, ⁼e	farm, farmyard
der Hahn, ⁼e	cock, rooster
der Hügel	hill
der Hund, -e	dog
der Landarbeiter	farm labourer
der Markt, ⁼e	market
der Wald, ⁼er	wood, forest

ESSENTIAL WORDS (f)

die Bäuerin ▢	lady farmer; farmer's wife; peasant
die Bauersfrau, -en	farmer's wife
die Ente, -n	duck
die Erde	earth, soil
die Gans, ⁼e	goose
die Henne, -n	hen
die (Heu)gabel, -n	pitchfork
die Katze, -n	cat
die Wiese, -n	meadow

ESSENTIAL WORDS (nt)

das Dorf, ⁼er	village
das Feld, -er	field
das Kalb, ⁼er	calf
das Land ⇔, ⁼er	land; country
das Tier, -e	animal

auf einem Bauernhof wohnen to live on a farm
Ferien auf dem Bauernhof farm holidays
der Bauer sorgt für die Tiere the farmer looks after the animals
die Felder pflügen to plough the fields
die Ernte einbringen to bring in the harvest *or* the crops
zur Erntezeit at harvest-time

IMPORTANT WORDS (m)	
der Bach, ̈-e ⌑	stream, brook
der Boden ◇, ̈:	ground, earth; floor; loft
der Bulle, -n	bull
der Lieferwagen	van
der Ochse, -n	ox
der Puter	turkey(-cock)
der Traktor, -en	tractor
der Weizen	wheat
der Zaun, Zäune	fence

IMPORTANT WORDS (f)	
die Feldmaus, (-mäuse)	fieldmouse
die Heide ◇, -n ⌑	heath
die Herde, -n	herd; flock
die Kuh, ̈-e	cow
die Landschaft, -en	countryside, scenery
die Landwirtschaft	agriculture, farming
die Milchkanne, -n	milk churn
die Pute, -n	turkey(-hen)

IMPORTANT WORDS (nt)	
das Bauernhaus, (-häuser)	farmhouse
das Gebäude	building
das Heu	hay
das Huhn, ̈-er	chicken, hen; (pl) poultry
das Hühnerhaus, (-häuser)	henhouse
das Korn, ̈-er	corn, grain
das Lamm, ̈-er	lamb
das Pferd, -e	horse
das Schaf, -e	sheep
das Schwein, -e	pig
das Stroh	straw

USEFUL WORDS (m)	
der Acker, ⸚	field
der Brunnen	well
der Dünger	dung, manure; fertilizer
der Eimer	bucket, pail
der Esel	donkey
der Graben, ⸚	ditch
der Hafer	oats (pl)
der Hase, -n	hare
der Haufen	heap, pile
der Heuboden, ⸚	hayloft
der Karren	cart
der Kuhstall, ⸚e	cowshed, byre
der Landwirt, -e	farmer
der Mähdrescher	combine harvester
der Mais ▷	maize
der Pferdestall, ⸚e	stable
der Pflug, ⸚e	plough
der Roggen	rye
der Schäfer	shepherd
der Schäferhund, -e	sheepdog, German shepherd
der Schlamm	mud
der Schuppen	shed
der Stall, ⸚e	stable; sty; (hen)house
der Stapel	pile
der Staub	dust
der Stier, -e	bull
der Teich, -e	pond
der Truthahn, ⸚e	turkey(-cock)
der Widder	ram

USEFUL WORDS (f)

die Ernte, -n	harvest, crop
die Erntezeit, -en	harvest (time)
die Furche, -n	furrow
die Garbe, -n	sheaf
die Gerste	barley
die Kleie	bran
die Leiter ◇, -n	ladder
die Scheune, -n	barn
die Vogelscheuche, -n	scarecrow
die Weide ◇, -n	pasture
die (Wind)mühle, -n	(wind)mill
die Ziege, -n	goat

USEFUL WORDS (nt)

das Gatter	gate; railing
das Geflügel	poultry
das Geschirr ◇, -e	harness
das Getreide	cereals, grain
das Küken	chicken, chick
das (Rind)vieh	cattle (*pl*), livestock
das Zugpferd, -e	carthorse

ESSENTIAL + IMPORTANT WORDS (m)

der Fische, -e	fish
der Goldfisch, -e	goldfish
der Moskito, -s	mosquito
der Schwanz, ⁻e	tail

USEFUL WORDS (m)

der Aal, -e	eel
der Floh, ⁻e	flea
der Flügel ⇨	wing
der Frosch, ⁻e	frog
der Hai(fisch), -e	shark
der Hecht, -e	pike
der Hering, -e	herring
der Hummer	lobster
der Kabeljau, -e *or* **-s**	cod
der Käfer	beetle
der Krebs, -e	crab; crayfish
der Lachs, -e	salmon
der Marienkäfer	ladybird
der Nachtfalter	moth
der Schellfisch, -e	haddock
der Schmetterling, -e	butterfly
der Stich, -e	sting
der Thunfisch, -e	tuna fish
der Tintenfisch, -e	(small) octopus, squid
der Weißfisch, -e	whiting
der Wurm, ⁻er	worm

ESSENTIAL + IMPORTANT WORDS (nt)

das Insekt, -en	insect
das Schalentier, -e	shellfish
das Wasser	water

im Wasser schwimmen to swim in the water
in der Luft fliegen to fly in the air
"Angeln verboten" "no fishing"

ESSENTIAL + IMPORTANT WORDS (f)

die Biene, -n	bee
die Fliege ⇨, -n 📖	fly
die Forelle, -n	trout
die Luft	air
die Sardine, -n	sardine
die Wespe, -n	wasp

USEFUL WORDS (f)

die Ameise, -n	ant
die Auster, -n	oyster
die Flosse, -n	fin
die Garnele, -n	shrimp; prawn
die Gespenstheuschrecke, -n	stick insect
die Grille, -n	cricket
die Heuschrecke, -n	grasshopper
die Hornisse, -n	hornet
die Kaulquappe, -n	tadpole
die Kiemen (pl)	gills
die Krabbe, -n	shrimp; prawn
die Krake, -n	octopus
die Languste, -n	crayfish
die Libelle ⇨, -n	dragonfly
die (Mies)muschel, -n	mussel
die Motte, -n	moth
die Mücke, -n	midge
die Qualle, -n	jellyfish
die Raupe, -n	caterpillar
die Schmeißfliege, -n	bluebottle
die Schuppe, -n	scale
die Seezunge, -n	sole
die Seidenraupe, -n	silkworm
die Spinne, -n	spider
die Wanze, -n	bug

stechen to sting
die Biene/die Wespe sticht the bee/the wasp stings

ESSENTIAL WORDS (m)	
der Alkohol	alcohol
der (Apfel)saft	(apple) juice
der Apfelstrudel	apple strudel
der Apfelwein	cider
der Appetit, -e	appetite
der Aufschnitt	cold meats
der Becher ⇨	mug; tumbler
die Chips (pl)	crisps
der Durst	thirst
der Eintopf ⌸	stew
der Essig	vinegar
der Fisch, -e	fish
der Honig	honey
der Hunger	hunger
der Imbiß, -sse	snack
der Joghurt, -s	yoghurt
der Kaffee	coffee
der Kakao, -s	cocoa
der Käse	cheese
der Keks, -e	biscuit
der Kellner	waiter
der Kuchen	cake
der Löffel	spoon
der Nachtisch, -e	dessert, sweet
der Pfeffer	pepper
der Reis	rice
der Salat ⇨, -e	salad
die Salzkartoffeln (pl) ⌸	boiled potatoes
der Schinken	ham
der Schnellimbiß, -sse ⌸	snack bar
der Senf, -e	mustard
der Sprudel	type of mineral water
der Tee	tea
der Teller	plate
der Tisch, -e	table
der Wein ⇨, -e	wine
ein Wiener Schnitzel	Wiener schnitzel

ESSENTIAL WORDS (m) (cont)

der Zucker	sugar
der Zuschlag, ⸚e	extra charge

essen to eat; **trinken** to drink
könnte ich bitte eine Cola haben? could I have a Coke please?
wie wär's mit einem Apfelsaft? do you fancy an apple juice?
schlucken to swallow; **schmecken** to taste (good)
das schmeckt ihm he likes it
schmeckt Ihnen der Wein? do you like the wine?
das schmeckt scheußlich! that tastes dreadful!
ich esse gern Käse I like (eating) cheese
ich trinke gern Tee I like (drinking) tea
ich mag Käse/Tee nicht, ich mag keinen Käse/Tee I don't like cheese/tea
ich esse lieber Brot/trinke lieber Bier I prefer bread/beer
hungrig sein, Hunger haben to be hungry
durstig sein, Durst haben to be thirsty
ich sterbe vor Hunger! I'm starving!
hast du schon gegessen? have you eaten yet?
frühstücken to have breakfast
vorbereiten to prepare; **kochen** to cook; **backen** to bake;
  braten to fry; **grillen** to grill; **würzen** to season
paniert in breadcrumbs
schneiden to cut; **streichen** to spread
einschenken to pour (tea etc)
bitten um to ask for; **reichen** to pass, hand on
Mahlzeit!, guten Appetit! enjoy your meal!
bedienen Sie sich!, nehmen Sie sich! help yourselves!
alkoholisch alcoholic; **alkoholfrei** non-alcoholic
den Tisch decken/abräumen to lay or set/clear the table
abwaschen, (das Geschirr) spülen to wash up, do the dishes
abtrocknen to dry the dishes

ESSENTIAL WORDS (f)

die Bedienung	service; service charge
die Bestellung, -en	order
die Bockwurst	*type of pork sausage*
die (Braten)soße	gravy
die Bratwurst	grilled *or* fried sausage
die Butter	butter
die Currywurst	curried sausage
die Dose, -n	box; tin, can
die Erfrischung, -en 🕮	refreshment
die Flasche, -n	bottle
die Frucht, ⸚e	(piece of) fruit
die Gabel, -n	fork
die Imbißstube, -n	snack bar
die Kaffeekanne, -n	coffee pot
die Kartoffel, -n	potato
die Kellnerin	waitress
die Leberwurst	liver sausage
die Limonade, -n	lemonade
die Mahlzeit, -en	meal
die Margarine	margarine
die Milch	milk
die Nachspeise, -n	dessert, sweet
die Pizza, -s	pizza
die kalte Platte, -n -n	cold meal
die Portion	portion, helping
die Praline, -n	(*individual*) chocolate
die Rechnung, -en	bill
die Sahne	cream
die Schlagsahne	whipped cream
die Schokolade, -n	chocolate
die Soße, -n	sauce
die Speisekarte, -n	menu
die Suppe	soup
die Tageskarte, -n	today's menu
die Tasse, -n	cup
die Teekanne, -n	teapot
die Torte, -n	flan, tart

ESSENTIAL WORDS (nt)

das Abendbrot	supper
das Abendessen	evening meal
das Bier, -e	beer
das Bonbon, -s	sweet, sweetie
das (Brat)hähnchen	(roast) chicken
das Brot, -e	bread; loaf
ein belegtes Brot, -n -e	open sandwich
das Brötchen	(bread) roll
das Butterbrot, -e	piece of bread and butter
das Café, -s	café
das Cola	Coke
ein Deutsches Beefsteak ⌐	hamburger
das Ei, -er	egg
das Eis ◇	ice cream
das Essen	meal
das Feuerzeug, -e	lighter
das Fleisch ◇	meat
das Frühstück, -e	breakfast
die Gemüse (pl)	vegetables
das Getränk, -e	drink
das Glas, ¨er	glass
das Gulasch	goulash
das Kalbfleisch	veal
das Kotelett, -e	chop
das Menü, -s	menu
das Messer	knife
das Mineralwasser	mineral water
das Mittagessen	lunch; dinner
das Obst	fruit
das Öl	oil
das Omelett, -s	omelette
das Picknick, -s or -e	picnic
das Pils ⌐	lager
die Pommes frites (pl)	chips, French fries
das Restaurant, -s	restaurant
das Rindfleisch	beef
das Rührei	scrambled egg

ESSENTIAL WORDS (f) (cont)	
die Untertasse, -n	saucer
die Wurst, ̈e	sausage (*large*)
die Zigarette, -n	cigarette
die Zigarre, -n	cigar

ESSENTIAL WORDS (nt) (cont)	
das Salz	salt
das Schnitzel	(veal) cutlet
das Schwarzbrot	rye bread
das Schweinefleisch	pork
das Spiegelei, -er	fried egg
das Steak, -s	steak
das Wasser	water
das Wirtshaus, (-häuser)	inn
das Würstchen	sausage (*small*)

IMPORTANT WORDS (m)	
der **Aschenbecher**	ashtray
der **Champagner**	champagne
der **Dessertlöffel**	dessert spoon
der **Einkaufswagen**	shopping trolley
der **Eßlöffel**	tablespoon
der **Geschmack, -̈e**	taste
der **Hamburger**	hamburger
der **Knödel**	dumpling
der **Kognak, -s**	brandy
der **Korken**	cork
der **Rindsbraten**	roast beef
der **Schnaps**	schnapps; spirits
der **Sekt, -e**	champagne
der **Stammtisch** ▢	*table for the regulars*
der **Strohhalm, -e**	(drinking) straw
der **Tabak**	tobacco
der **Teelöffel**	teaspoon
der **Toast, -s**	toast
der **Whisky, -s**	whisky

rauchen to smoke
danke, ich rauche nicht no thanks, I don't smoke
"Rauchen verboten" "no smoking"
um Feuer bitten to ask for a light
anzünden to light up
ich versuche, das Rauchen aufzugeben I'm trying to give
up smoking

FOOD and DRINK

IMPORTANT WORDS (f)

die **Auswahl** (an + *dat*)	choice (of)
die **Getränkekarte** 📖	wine list
die **Kneipe**, -n	pub
die **Marmelade**, -n	jam
die **Mayonnaise**	mayonnaise
die **Meeresfrüchte** (*pl*)	seafood, shellfish
die **Nudeln** (*pl*)	pasta, noodles
die **Orangenmarmelade**, -n	marmalade
die **Salami**	salami
die **Salatsoße**	salad dressing
die **Schale**, -n	bowl
die **Scheibe**, -n	slice
die **Schenke**, -n 📖	inn
die **Schüssel**, -n	bowl, dish
die **Theke**, -n	bar; counter
die **Vanillesoße**	custard
die **Vorspeise**, -n	hors d'œuvre, starter
die **Wirtschaft**	pub

IMPORTANT WORDS (nt)

das **Gericht** ◇, -e	dish, course
das **Geschirr** ◇	dishes, crockery
das **Hauptgericht**, -e	main course
das **Lammfleisch**	lamb
das **Mus**	purée
das **Rezept** ◇, -e	recipe
das **Sandwich**, -es	sandwich
das **Tablett**, -e	tray
das **Trinkgeld**, -er	tip

bestellen to order
können Sie mir etwas empfehlen? what do you
recommend?

USEFUL WORDS (m)	
der Eiswürfel	ice cube
der Kaffeefilter	coffee-maker
der Krug (¨e) Wasser	jug of water
der Pfannkuchen	pancake
der Rahm	cream
der (Schinken)speck	bacon
der Wackelpeter	jelly
der Weinbrand	brandy
der Zwieback	toast (*in packets*)

USEFUL WORDS (f)	
die Büchse, -n	tin, can
die Eisdiele, -n	ice cream parlour
die Frikadelle, -n	rissole
die Konserven (*pl*)	preserved foods
die Niere, -n	kidney
die Pfeife, -n	pipe
die Serviette, -n	napkin, serviette
die Thermosflasche, -n	flask

USEFUL WORDS (nt)	
das Geflügel	poultry
das Kartoffelpüree	mashed potatoes
das Korinthenbrötchen	bun
das Mehl, -e	flour
das Streichholz, ¨er	match
das Tischtuch, ¨er	tablecloth
das Tutti Frutti	trifle
das Wild	game (*meat*)

ESSENTIAL WORDS (m)

der Ausflug, ¨-e	outing, trip
der Besuch, -e	visit; visitor
der Brieffreund, -e	penfriend
der Computer, -s	computer
der Fan, -s; der Fanatiker	fan
der Film, -e	film
der (Foto)apparat, -e	camera
der Freund, -e	friend; boyfriend
der Jugendklub, -s	youth club
der Kassettenrecorder	cassette recorder
der Plattenspieler	record player
der Sänger	singer
der Schlager	hit (record)
der Spaziergang, ¨-e	walk
der Sport, -e	sport
der Tanz, ¨-e	dance
der Verein, -e	club
der Zoo, -s	zoo

ESSENTIAL WORDS (f)

die Brieffreundin	penfriend
die Diskothek, -en	disco
die Einladung, -en ⌂	invitation
die Eintrittskarte, -n ⌂	(admission) ticket
die Fotografie, -n	photograph; photography
die Freizeit	free time, spare time
die Freundin	friend; girlfriend
die Kassette, -n	cassette
die Langspielplatte, -n	LP
die Musik	music
die Sängerin	singer
die (Schall)platte, -n	record
die (Spiel)karte, -n	(playing) card
die Stereoanlage, -en	stereo (system)
die Zeitschrift, -en	magazine
die Zeitung, -en	newspaper

ESSENTIAL WORDS (nt)

das Band ⋄, ⁻er	(recording) tape
das Fernsehen	watching television
das Hobby, -s	hobby
das Interesse, -n	interest
das Kartenspiel, -e	game of cards; pack of cards
das Kino, -s	cinema
das Konzert, -e	concert
das Lesen	reading
das Magazin, -e	magazine
das Museum, Museen	museum
das Programm ⋄, -e	(TV) programme
das Radio, -s	radio
das Singen	singing
das Spiel ⋄, -e	game
das Taschengeld	pocket money
das Theater, -s	theatre
das Transistor(radio), -s	transistor (radio)
das Wandern	hiking, rambling
das Wochenende	weekend

in meiner Freizeit in my free *or* spare time
die Zeit verbringen, etw zu tun to spend time doing sth
am Wochenende at the weekend(s)
sich ausruhen to rest; **beschließen** to decide; **treffen** to
  meet
amüsiere dich gut! enjoy yourself, have fun!
es hat mir wirklich gut gefallen I really liked it
ausgezeichnet! excellent!; **toll!** terrific!
einen Spaziergang machen to go for a walk
fernsehen to watch television
Radio hören to listen to the radio
umschalten to turn over, change channels
Platten hören to play records; **aufnehmen** to record
fotografieren to take photos (of); **knipsen** to snap
lesen to read; **schreiben** to write; **sammeln** to collect;
malen to paint; **zeichnen** to draw

IMPORTANT WORDS (m)	
der Karneval, -e *or* -s 📖	carnival
der Krimi, -s	thriller, detective story
der Nachtklub, -s	night club
der Pfadfinder	boy scout
der Roman, -e	novel
der Treffpunkt, -e 📖	meeting place
der Walkman ®	personal stereo, Walkman ®

IMPORTANT WORDS (f)	
die Aufnahme, -n	shot (*photo*); recording
die Ausstellung, -en	exhibition
die Besichtigung, -en 📖	visit
die (Briefmark)sammlung, -en	(stamp) collection
die Ermäßigung, -en	reduction
die Freizeitbeschäftigung, -en	hobby, spare-time activity
die Führung, -en 📖	conducted tour
die Illustrierte, -n 📖	magazine
die Messe ◇, -n 📖	fair; mass
die Nachrichten (*pl*) 📖	news, newscast
die Pfadfinderin	girl scout
die Sendung, -en	transmission, programme
die Unterhaltung, -en	entertainment; talk
die Verabredung, -en	date, appointment
die Videokassette, -n	video (cassette)
die Wanderung, -en	walk, hike

IMPORTANT WORDS (nt)	
das Dia, -s	slide, transparency
das Mitglied, -er	member
das Nähen	sewing
das Schach	chess
das Stricken	knitting
das Taschenbuch, ̈-er 📖	paperback
das Videogerät, -e	video (recorder)

USEFUL WORDS (m)	
der Fortsetzungsroman, -e	serial
der Musikautomat, -en	jukebox
der Spielautomat, -en	slot machine
der Wettbewerb, -e	competition
der Zeitvertreib, -e	pastime

USEFUL WORDS (f)	
die Begeisterung	enthusiasm
die Compact-Disc	compact disc
die Familienserie, -n	soap opera
die Filmkamera, -s	cine camera
die Hitliste	charts, top twenty
die Maxi-Single, -s	12-inch single
die Party, -s or Parties	party
die Schlagerparade	charts, hit parade
die Stickerei	embroidery
die Versammlung, -en	meeting, gathering

USEFUL WORDS (nt)	
das Album, Alben	album
die Comics (pl)	cartoons, comic strips
das Damespiel	draughts
das Feriendorf, ¨er	holiday camp
das Ferienlager	school camp
das Kreuzworträtsel	crossword (puzzle)
das Lied, -er	song
das Modell, -e	model, kit
das Rollbrett, -er or	
das Skateboard, -s	skateboard

ich interessiere mich für (+acc) I am interested in ...
eine Party geben to have a party
hast du Lust, zu meiner Party zu kommen? do you fancy
   coming to my party?
wir kommen jeden Freitag zusammen we meet or get
   together every Friday

ESSENTIAL + IMPORTANT WORDS (m)

der Apfel, ⸚	apple
der Apfelbaum, (-bäume)	apple tree
der Birnenbaum, (-bäume)	pear tree
der Obstbaum, (-bäume)	fruit tree
der Obstgarten, ⸚	orchard
der Pfirsich, -e	peach
der Pfirsichbaum, (-bäume)	peach tree
der Wein ⟡, Weinstöcke	vine

ESSENTIAL + IMPORTANT WORDS (f)

die Apfelsine, -n	orange
die Banane, -n	banana; banana tree
die Birne ⟡, -n	pear
die Erdbeere, -n	strawberry
eine Frucht, ⸚e	(a piece of) fruit
die Himbeere, -n	raspberry
die Kirsche, -n	cherry
die Melone ⟡, -n	melon
die Olive, -n	olive
die Orange, -n	orange; orange tree
die Pflaume, -n	plum
die Schale	skin; peel; shell
die (Wein)traube, -n	grape; bunch of grapes
die Zitrone, -n	lemon

ESSENTIAL WORDS (nt)

das Kompott, -e	stewed fruit
das Obst	fruit
das Stück Obst	piece of fruit

reif ripe; **unreif** not ripe
süß sweet; **bitter** sour, bitter
hart hard; **weich** soft; **saftig** juicy
pflücken to pick; **sammeln** to gather
essen to eat; **beißen** to bite
blaue/grüne Trauben black/green grapes

USEFUL WORDS (m)	
der Granatapfel, ¨	pomegranate
der Kern, -e	pip, stone (in fruit)
der Nußbaum, (-bäume)	walnut tree
der Rhabarber	rhubarb
der Walnußbaum, (-bäume)	walnut tree
der Weinberg, -e	vineyard
der Weinstock, ¨e	vine

USEFUL WORDS (f)	
die Ananas, - or -se	pineapple
die Aprikose, -n	apricot; apricot tree
die Backpflaume, -n	prune
die Beere, -n	berry
die Brombeere, -n	blackberry, bramble
die Dattel, -n	date
die Erdnuß, (-nüsse)	peanut
die Feige, -n	fig
die Grapefruit	grapefruit
die Haselnuß, (-nüsse)	hazelnut
die Heidelbeere, -n	bilberry
die Johannisbeere, -n	redcurrant
die schwarze Johannisbeere, -n -n	blackcurrant
die Kastanie, -n	chestnut; chestnut tree
die Kiwi(frucht), -s and (¨e)	kiwi (fruit)
die Kokosnuß, (-nüsse)	coconut
die Mandarine, -n	tangerine
die Nuß, Nüsse	nut
die Pampelmuse, -n	grapefruit
die Passionsfrucht, ¨e	passion fruit
die Stachelbeere, -n	gooseberry
die Traube, -n	grape; bunch of grapes
die Traubenlese, -n	grape harvest, vintage
die Walnuß, (-nüsse)	walnut
die (Wein)rebe, -n	vine
die Zwetsch(g)e, -n	plum

ESSENTIAL WORDS (m)

der Fernsehapparat, -e *or*	
der Fernseher	television set
der Fernsprecher 🕮	telephone
der Herd, -e 🕮	cooker
der Kassettenrecorder	cassette recorder
der Kleiderschrank, ⁻e	wardrobe
der Kühlschrank, ⁻e	fridge, refrigerator
der Plattenspieler	record player
der Raum ⋄, Räume 🕮	room
der Schrank, ⁻e	cupboard
der Sessel	armchair
der Stuhl, ⁻e	chair
der Tisch, -e	table
der Wecker	alarm clock

ESSENTIAL WORDS (f)

die Lampe, -n	lamp
die Stehlampe, -n 🕮	standard lamp, floor lamp
die Stereoanlage, -n	stereo system
die Uhr ⋄, -en	clock
die Waschmaschine, -n	washing machine

ESSENTIAL WORDS (nt)

das Bett, -en	bed
das Bild, -er	picture, painting
das Haus, Häuser	house
das Sofa, -s	settee, couch
das Telefon, -e	telephone
das Zimmer	room

fernsehen to watch television
im Fernsehen on television
telefonieren to telephone
anrufen to phone, call
Musik hören to listen to music
programmieren to programme

IMPORTANT WORDS (m)

der Elektroherd, -e	electric cooker
der Gasherd, -e	gas cooker
der Nachttisch, -e	bedside table
der Ofen, ⸚	oven
der Spiegel	mirror
der Stecker	plug
der Strom ▷	(electricity) current
der Videorecorder	video recorder
der Walkman ®	personal stereo, Walkman ®

IMPORTANT WORDS (f)

die Kuckucksuhr, -en	cuckoo clock
die Schreibmaschine, -n	typewriter
die Spülmaschine, -n	dishwasher
die Steckdose, -n	(wall) socket

IMPORTANT WORDS (nt)

das (Bücher)regal, -e	bookcase, bookshelves
das Klavier, -e	piano
die Möbel (pl)	furniture
das Möbel(stück)	piece of furniture
das Regal, -e	(set of) shelves
das Transistor(radio), -s	transistor (radio)
das Videogerät, -e	video (recorder)

ein Zimmer möblieren to furnish a room
ein möbliertes Zimmer a furnished room
bequem comfortable; **unbequem** uncomfortable
in dem Zimmer ist es sehr eng the room is very cramped
den Tisch decken/abräumen to lay or set/to clear the table
das Bett machen to make the bed
ins Bett gehen, zu Bett gehen to go to bed

USEFUL WORDS (m)

der Anrufbeantworter	telephone answering machine
der Backofen, ⸚	oven
der Bücherschrank, ⸚e	bookcase
der Couchtisch, -e	coffee table
der Eßtisch, -e	dining table
der Frisiertisch, -e	dressing table
der Heizofen, ⸚	fire, heater
der Hocker	stool
die Kleiderhaken (pl)	coat hooks, coat rack
der Lehnsessel or	
der Lehnstuhl, ⸚e	armchair
der Mikrowellenherd, -e	microwave oven
der Möbelwagen	furniture van, removal van
der Nachtstrom(heiz)ofen	(night-)storage heater
der Rahmen	frame
der Satz ◇, (⸚e) Tische	nest of tables
der Schaukelstuhl, ⸚e	rocking chair
der Schirmständer	umbrella stand
der Schnellkochtopf, ⸚e	pressure cooker
der Schreibtisch, -e	writing desk
der Schutzengel	baby's highchair
der Sekretär ◇, -e	bureau, writing desk
der Staubsauger	vacuum cleaner, Hoover®
der Teewagen	trolley
der Umzug ◇, ⸚e	removal

sitzen to sit, be sitting
sich setzen to sit down
sich hinlegen to lie down
sich ausruhen to rest
ein Zimmer ausräumen to clear out a room
ein Zimmer aufräumen or **in Ordnung bringen** to tidy up a room
(die Möbel) umräumen to move the furniture around
putzen to clean; **abstauben** to dust; **staubsaugen** to hoover

---

USEFUL WORDS (f)

die Anrichte, -n	dresser; sideboard
die Einrichtung	furnishings (*pl*)
die Kommode, -n	chest of drawers
die Matratze, -n	mattress
die Nähmaschine, -n	sewing machine
die Satellitenantenne, -n	satellite dish
die Schublade, -n	drawer
die Spedition	removal firm
die Standuhr, -en	grandfather clock
die Strickmaschine, -n	knitting machine
die Tiefkühltruhe, -n	freezer, deep freeze
die Truhe, -n	chest, trunk
die Video-kamera, -s	video camera
die Wäscheschleuder	spin dryer
die Wiege, -n	cradle

USEFUL WORDS (nt)

das Bord ⬥, -e	shelf
das Etagenbett, -en	bunk bed
das Gemälde	painting, picture
das Gerät, -e	appliance
das Kinderbettchen	cot
das Rollo, -s *or*	
das Rouleau, -s	blind
das Schubfach, ¨er	drawer
das schnurlose Telefon	cordless telephone
das Tonbandgerät, -e	tape recorder

elektrisch electric
anmachen, einschalten to turn *or* switch on
ausmachen, ausschalten to turn *or* switch off
es funktioniert nicht it's not working
heizen to heat
gemütlich comfortable, cosy

Antwerpen (*nt*)	Antwerp
der **Ärmelkanal**	the English Channel
der **Atlantik,**	
der **Atlantische Ozean**	the Atlantic (Ocean)
Basel (*nt*)	Basle
Bayern (*nt*)	Bavaria
Berlin (*nt*)	Berlin
der **Bodensee**	Lake Constance
die **britischen Inseln** (*fpl*)	the British Isles
Brüssel (*nt*)	Brussels
die **Donau**	the Danube
Edinburg (*nt*)	Edinburgh
Elsaß (*nt*)	Alsace
der **Ferne Osten**	the Far East
Genf (*nt*)	Geneva
der **Genfer See**	Lake Geneva
Gent (*nt*)	Ghent
der **Große Ozean**	the Pacific Ocean
Den Haag (*nt*)	The Hague
Hannover (*nt*)	Hanover
Kairo (*nt*)	Cairo
die **Kanalinseln** (*fpl*)	the Channel Islands
Köln (*nt*)	Cologne
Korsika (*nt*)	Corsica
Lissabon (*nt*)	Lisbon
Lothringen (*nt*)	Lorraine
Mailand (*nt*)	Milan
Mallorca (*nt*)	Majorca
das **Mittelmeer**	the Mediterranean
die **Mosel**	Moselle
Moskau (*nt*)	Moscow
München (*nt*)	Munich
der **Nahe Osten**	the Middle East
die **Nordee**	the North Sea
die **Ostsee**	the Baltic Sea
der **Pazifik,**	
der **Pazifische Ozean**	the Pacific (Ocean)
Peking (*nt*)	Beijing
die **Pyrenäen** (*nt*)	the Pyrenees

der **Rhein**	the Rhine
Rom (*nt*)	Rome
der **Schwarzwald**	the Black Forest
die **Seine**	the Seine
der **Stille Ozean**	the Pacific Ocean
die **Themse**	the Thames
Venedig (*nt*)	Venice
der **Vesuv**	Mount Vesuvius
Warschau (*nt*)	Warsaw
Wien (*nt*)	Vienna
die **Wolga**	the Volga

Athener, -in an Athenian
Bas(e)ler, -in a person from Basle
Bayer, -in a Bavarian
Böhme, Böhmin a person from Bohemia
Elsässer, -in a person from Alsace, an Alsatian
Flame, Flamin *or* **Flämin** a person from Flanders, a Fleming
Friese, Friesin a person from Frisia, a Frisian
Hamburger, -in a person from Hamburg
Hannoveraner, -in a person from Hanover, a Hanoverian
Hesse, Hessin a person from Hesse
Indianer, -in a (Red) Indian
Londoner, -in a Londoner
Moskauer, -in a person from Moscow, a Muskovite
Münch(e)ner, -in a person from Munich
Neapolitaner, -in a Neapolitan
Pariser, -in a Parisian
Preuße, Preußin a Prussian
Rheinländer, -in a Rheinlander
Römer, -in a person from Rome, a Roman
Sachse, Sächsin a person from Saxony
Schwabe, Schwäbin a person from Swabia
Tiroler, -in a person from the Tyrol
Venezianer, -in a Venetian
Westfale, Westfälin a Westphalian
Wiener, -in a person from Vienna, a Viennese

GREETINGS AND FAREWELLS

guten Tag! good day, hello; good afternoon
guten Morgen! good morning
guten Abend! good evening
gute Nacht! good night (*when going to bed*)
auf Wiedersehen! goodbye
auf Wiederhören! goodbye (*on phone*)
he! hi!; Tschüs! Servus hello; goodbye
wie geht's?; wie geht es Ihnen? how are things?
gut, danke; es geht mir gut, danke very well, thank you
sehr angenehm pleased to meet you
bis später see you later
bis morgen see you tomorrow

BEST WISHES

ich gratuliere! congratulations!
alles Gute all the best, best wishes
herzliche Glückwünsche congratulations, best wishes
alles Gute zum Geburtstag happy birthday
alles Gute zum Hochzeitstag congratulations on your
  wedding day
viel Glück all the best; the best of luck
fröhliche Weihnachten merry Christmas
gutes neues Jahr happy New Year
guten Appetit, Mahlzeit! have a good meal, enjoy your meal
Prost! cheers; **zum Wohl!** good health!
Gesundheit! bless you! (*after a sneeze*)
viel Spaß! have a good time, enjoy yourself *etc*
schlaf gut! sleep well
gut geschlafen? did you sleep well?

grüßen, begrüßen to greet, welcome
sich verabschieden to say goodbye, take one's leave
(sich) vorstellen to introduce (oneself)

SURPRISE

ach du meine Güte oh my goodness, oh dear
so?, wirklich? really?
so, so! well, well!; **ach so!** oh I see!
na, so etwas! you don't say!
wie? what?
was für ein Glück! what a piece of luck!

POLITENESS

bitte please, excuse me
danke thank you; **nein danke** no thank you
ja bitte, bitte ja yes please
tu das ja nicht don't do that
danke, schön, danke sehr, vielen Dank thank you very
   much, many thanks
bitte schön, bitte sehr don't mention it
gern geschehen my pleasure, don't mention it
entschuldigen Sie, Entschuldigung excuse me; I'm sorry
verzeihen Sie, Verzeihung (*formal*) I'm sorry, I beg your
   pardon
pardon excuse me, I'm sorry
es macht nichts it doesn't matter
(wie) bitte? (I beg your) pardon?
na bitte, bitte schön, bitte sehr there you are
mit Vergnügen with pleasure
machen Sie keine Umstände don't go to any trouble

WARNINGS

Achtung! watch out!; **Vorsicht!** be careful!
paß auf! look out!, watch out!
halten Sie! stop!
Feuer! fire!; **halten den Dieb!** stop thief!
Ruhe!, ruhig! be quiet!; **halt den Mund!** shut up!
herein! come in!; **heraus!** get out!
beeile dich! hurry up!; **hau ab!** clear off!
geh mir aus dem Weg! get out of my way!

AGREEMENT and DISAGREEMENT

ja yes; **doch** yes (*when contradictory*)
nein no
jawohl yes indeed
natürlich of course
natürlich nicht, aber nein of course not
nicht wahr? isn't that right?
in Ordnung O.K., all right
gut good, O.K.
na gut, also gut O.K. then, all right then
schön fine
einverstanden! agreed!
genau, ganz recht exactly
desto besser so much the better
ich habe nichts dagegen I don't mind *or* object
das ist mir gleich *or* **einerlei** *or* **egal** I don't mind, it's all the
    same to me, it's all one to me
das stimmt that's right
das stimmt nicht that doesn't make sense
im Gegenteil on the contrary
nie!, um nichts in der Welt! never!, not on your life!
kümmern Sie sich um Ihre eigenen Dinge! mind your own
    business!
nieder mit ... down with ...

DISTRESS

Hilfe! help!
ach je! oh dear!
ach!, o weh! alas!
was ist los (mit dir)? what's the matter (with you)?, what's wrong (with you)?
leider (nicht) unfortunately (not)
es tut mir leid I'm sorry
es tut mir wirklich leid I'm really sorry
wie schade what a pity
das ist Pech it's a shame, that's bad luck
verflixt (nochmal)! blow!, drat!, dash it!
verflucht!, verdammt! damn!
ich habe es satt I'm fed up with it
ich kann ihn nicht ausstehen I can't stand him
was soll ich tun? what shall I do?
wie ärgerlich! what a nuisance!, how annoying!

OTHER EXPRESSIONS
---

vielleicht perhaps, maybe
ich weiß nicht I don't know
(ich habe) keine Ahnung (I've) no idea
ich weiß da nicht Bescheid I don't know (anything about it)
ich weiß nicht genau I don't know exactly
das kann ich mir vorstellen I can believe that
Schade! shame!
mein Gott! good Lord!
(ach) du lieber Himmel! (good) heavens!, goodness gracious!
prima! great!
klasse! terrific!, marvellous!
machen Sie sich keine Sorgen don't worry
aber wirklich! well really!
du machst wohl Witze you must be joking *or* kidding!
so eine Frechheit! what a nerve *or* cheek!
armes Ding! poor thing!

ESSENTIAL WORDS (m)

der Arzt, ̈-e	doctor, G.P.
der Durchfall	diarrhoea
die Kopfschmerzen (pl)	a headache
Kranke(r), -n	patient
der Krankenwagen	ambulance
der Zahnarzt, ̈-e	dentist

ESSENTIAL WORDS (f)

die Allergie, -n	allergy
die Ärztin	doctor, G.P.
die Erkältung, -en	cold; chill
die Erste Hilfe	first aid
die Gesundheit	health
die Grippe	flu, influenza
die Klinik, -en	hospital, clinic
die Krankenschwester, -n	nurse
die Krankheit, -en	illness
die Lebensgefahr	danger (to life)
die Medizin	(science of) medicine
die Pille, -n	pill
die Tablette, -n	tablet, pill
die Temperatur, -en	temperature
die Verstopfung	constipation

ESSENTIAL WORDS (nt)

das Fieber	fever, (high) temperature
das Heimweh	homesickness
das Kopfweh	headache
das Krankenhaus, (-häuser)	hospital

krank ill; **gesund** healthy; **wohl** well
schwach weak; **atemlos** breathless
müde tired; **schwindlig** dizzy; **blaß** pale
sich erkälten to catch cold
husten to cough; **niesen** to sneeze
schwitzen to sweat

IMPORTANT WORDS (m)

der Apotheker	(dispensing) chemist
der Atem	breath
die Bauchschmerzen (pl)	stomach-ache
der E 111-Schein	E 111 form
der Gips	plaster; plaster of Paris
der Gipsverband, ¨e	plaster (cast)
die Halsschmerzen (pl)	a sore throat
der Husten	cough
der Krankenschein, -e	health insurance card
der Kurort, -e □	health resort
die Magenschmerzen (pl)	stomach-ache
der Operationssaal, (-säle)	operating theatre
der Patient, -en	patient
der Schmerz, -en	pain, ache
der Schnupfen	cold (in the head)
der Schweiß	sweat
der Tod, -e	death
der Tropfen	drop
der Verband, ¨e	bandage, dressing
die Zahnschmerzen (pl)	toothache

IMPORTANT WORDS (f)

die Feuerwehr, -en	fire brigade
die Krankenkasse	health insurance
die Kur, -en □	cure, treatment
die Operation, -en	operation
die Patientin	patient
die Ruhe ◇	rest
die Sorge, -n	care, worry
die Spritze, -n	syringe; injection
die Untersuchung ◇, -en	medical examination
die Verletzung, -en	injury
die Wunde, -n	wound
die Zunge, -n	tongue

IMPORTANT WORDS (nt)

das AIDS, Aids	AIDS, aids
das Aspirin	aspirin
das Blut	blood
das Heftpflaster	sticking plaster
das Leiden	complaint, condition
das Medikament	medicine
das Rezept ⬦, -e	prescription
das Thermometer	thermometer

USEFUL WORDS (f)

die Abmagerungskur	(*slimming*) diet
die Bandage, -n	(elastic) bandage
die Blase, -n	blister; bladder
die Blinddarmentzündung	appendicitis
die Blutübertragung	blood transfusion
die Diät, -en	(special) diet
die Droge, -n	drug
die Epidemie, -n	epidemic
die Genesung	recovery
die Kraft, ⁻e	strength, power
die Krücke, -n	crutch
die Mandelentzündung	tonsillitis
die Masern (*pl*)	measles
die Migräne	migraine
die Narbe, -n	scar
die Poliklinik, -en	health centre
die Röntgenaufnahme, -n	X-ray
die Röteln (*pl*)	German measles
die Salbe, -n	ointment, cream
die Schiene, -n	splint
die Schlinge, -n	sling
die Station ⬦, -en	ward
die Tragbahre, -n	stretcher
die Übelkeit	sickness, vomiting
die Watte	cotton wool
die Windpocken (*pl*)	chickenpox

USEFUL WORDS (m)

der Bazillus, Bazillen	germ
der Herzanfall, ⸚e	heart attack
der Heuschnupfen	hayfever
der Hitzschlag	heatstroke
HIV-Infizierte(r)	person who is HIV-positive
der Kratzer	scratch
der Mumps	mumps
der Puls	pulse
der Rückfall, ⸚e	relapse
der Schlaganfall, ⸚e	stroke
der Schock	shock
der Sonnenstich	sunstroke
der Stich, -e	sting
der Typhus	typhoid

USEFUL WORDS (nt)

das Altersheim, -e	old people's home
das Antibiotikum, -ka	antibiotic
das Erbrechen	sickness, vomiting
das Gift, -e	poison
das Sprechzimmer	surgery, consulting room

fallen, stürzen to fall; **brechen** to break
können Sie mir helfen? can you help me?
ich bin mit dem Auto verunglückt I've had an accident with the car
was fehlt Ihnen? what's the matter with you?
es blutet it's bleeding; **es tut weh** it hurts
verletzt injured, hurt
verwundet wounded
sich übergeben to vomit, be sick
untersuchen to examine; **verbinden** to bandage
pflegen to look after, nurse
gute Besserung! get well soon!
sich erholen to recover
sterben to die; **tot** dead

ESSENTIAL WORDS (m)

der (Farb)fernseher	(colour) television set
der Gast, ¨e	guest
der Gastof, ¨e	hotel, inn
der Kellner	waiter
der Koch, ¨e	cook
der Koffer	case, suitcase
der Lift, -e or -s	lift
der Notausgang, ¨e ⌑	emergency exit
der Reisepaß, ¨sse	passport
der Schalter ◇	switch
der Scheck, -s	cheque
der Schlüssel	key
der Stock, Stockwerke	floor, storey
der Tag, -e	day
der Weinkellner	wine waiter
der Zuschlag, ¨e	extra charge

ESSENTIAL WORDS (f)

die Anmeldung ⌑	registration
die Antwort, -en	answer
die Bar, -s	bar
die Bedienung	service; service charge
die Dusche, -n	shower
die Halbpension	half board
die Kellnerin	waitress
die Köchin	cook
die Mahlzeit, -en	meal
die Nacht, ¨e	night
die Pension, -en	guest-house, boarding house
die Rechnung, -en	bill
die Tasche ◇, -n	bag
die Toilette, -n	toilet
die Übernachtung mit Frühstück	bed and breakfast
die Vollpension	full board
die Woche, -n	week

ESSENTIAL + IMPORTANT WORDS (nt)	
das Badezimmer	bathroom
das Café, -s	café
das Doppelbett, -en	double bed
das Doppelzimmer	double room
das Einzelzimmer	single room
das Erdgeschoß, -sse	ground floor, ground level
das (Farb)fernsehen	(colour) television
das Formular, -e 📖	form
das Freibad, ̈-er	open-air swimming pool
das Fremdenzimmer 📖	guest room
das Frühstück, -e	breakfast
das Gasthaus, (-häuser)	inn, hotel
das Gepäck	luggage
das Hotel, -s	hotel
das Kleingeld	small change
das Mittagessen	lunch
das Restaurant, -s	restaurant
das Speisezimmer	dining room
das Telefon, -e	telephone
das Treppenhaus, (-häuser)	staircase
das Wirtshaus, (-haüser)	inn
das Zimmer	room
das Zimmermädchen	chambermaid

einpacken to get packed; **auspacken** to get unpacked
ich habe schon gebucht I have already booked
eine Reservierung bestätigen to confirm a reservation
sich in einem Hotel anmelden to book in at a hotel
ich möchte hier übernachten I'd like a room for the night here
ein Formular ausfüllen to fill in a form
3 Tage bleiben to stay for 3 days

IMPORTANT WORDS (m)

der **Aufenthalt**, -e	stay
der **Aufzug**, ¨-e	lift
der **Balkon** ◇, -s *or* -e	balcony
der **Blick**, -e	view
der **Empfangschef**, -s ▭	receptionist, reception clerk
der **Feuerlöscher** ▭	fire extinguisher
der **Gepäckträger** ◇	porter
der **Hotelier**, -s	hotelier, hotel-keeper
der **Prospekt**, -e	leaflet, brochure
der **Reiseführer** ▭	guide-book; travel guide (*person*)
der **Reiseleiter** ▭	travel courier
der **Stern**, -e	star

IMPORTANT WORDS (f)

die **Aussicht**, -en ▭	view
die **Empfangsdame**, -n	receptionist
die **Garderobe** ◇, -n	cloakroom
die **Gaststätte**, -n	restaurant; pub
die **Kneipe**, -n	pub
die **Mehrwertsteuer** ▭	value added tax
die **Nummer**, -n	number
die **Rezeption**	reception, reception desk
die **Terrasse**, -n	terrace
die **Unterkunft**, (-künfte)	accommodation
die **Veranstaltung**, -en	organization

USEFUL WORDS (m)

der Brand, ¨-e	fire
der (Gast)wirt, -e	owner, innkeeper, landlord
der Ober	waiter
der Oberkellner	head waiter

USEFUL WORDS (f)

die (Gast)wirtin	owner, innkeeper, landlady
die Vorhalle, -n	foyer

USEFUL WORDS (nt)

das Foyer	foyer
das Kellergeschoß	basement
das Schwimmbecken	swimming pool
das Stockwerk, -e	floor, storey
das Trinkgeld, -er	tip
das Wechselgeld	change
das Zweibettzimmer	twin-bedded room

ich möchte ein Zimmer mit Dusche/mit Bad I'd like a
  room with a shower/with a bath
was kostet es?, wie teuer ist es? how much is it?
das ist ziemlich teuer that is rather expensive
das Zimmer hat Aussicht *or* **Blick auf den Strand** the room
  overlooks the beach
im ersten/zehnten Stock on the first/tenth floor
im Erdgeschoß on the ground floor, on ground level
Herr Ober! waiter!
Fräulein! excuse me, miss!
"Bedienung inbegriffen" "service included"
"inklusive Bedienung" "inclusive of service"
"Sie brauchen nur zu klingeln" "just ring"
"Zimmer frei" "vacancies"

ESSENTIAL WORDS (m)

der Bungalow, -s	bungalow
der Flur, -e ▢	(entrance) hall
der (Fuß)boden, ̈ ▢	floor
der Garten, ̈	garden
der Haushalt ▢	household
der Hof, ̈e	yard
der Keller	cellar
der Mieter	tenant
der Park, -s	public park
der Parkplatz, ̈e	parking space
der Raum ◇, Räume ▢	room; space
der Schlüssel	key
der Speisesaal, (-säle)	dining room
der Stein, -e	stone
der Stock, Stockwerke	floor, storey

ESSENTIAL WORDS (f)

die Adresse, -n	address
die Dusche, -n	shower
die Familie, -n	family
die Garage, -n	garage
die Hausfrau, -en	housewife
die Haustür, -en	front door
die Küche, -n	kitchen; cooking
die Miete, -n ▢	rent
die Stadt, ̈e	town
die Straße, -n	street, road
die Toilette, -n	toilet
die Treppe, -n	stairs, staircase
die Tür, -en	door
die Wand, ̈e	(*inside*) wall
die Wohnung, -en	flat

in der Stadt/auf dem Lande wohnen to live in the town/in
the country
mieten to rent; **bauen** to build; **besitzen** to own

ESSENTIAL WORDS (nt)	
das Bad ◇, ⁼er; das Badezimmer	bathroom
das Doppelhaus, (-häuser)	semi-detached (house)
das Dorf, ⁼er	village
das Einfamilienhaus, (-häuser)	detached house
das Erdgeschoß, -sse	ground floor, ground level
das Eßzimmer	dining room
das Fenster	window
das Haus, Häuser	house
das Klo (Klosett)	toilet, loo
das Reihenhaus, (-häuser)	terraced house
das Schlafzimmer	bedroom
das Schloß ◇, ⁼sser	lock
das Treppenhaus ▢	staircase
das Wohnzimmer	lounge, living room
das Zentrum, Zentren	centre
das Zimmer	room

IMPORTANT WORDS (nt)	
das Dach, ⁼er	roof
das Gebäude ▢	building
das Gebiet, -e ▢	area
das Hochhaus, (-häuser) ▢	high-rise (building)
die Möbel (pl)	furniture
das Möbel(stück)	piece of furniture
das Parkett ◇, -e	wooden or parquet floor
das Tor ◇, -e	gate

USEFUL WORDS (nt)	
das Arbeitszimmer	study
das Dachfenster	skylight
das Gastzimmer	spare room, guest room
das Kellergeschoß, -sse	basement
das Oberlicht, -er	skylight
das Stockwerk, -e	floor, storey

IMPORTANT WORDS (m)

der Aufzug, -̈e	lift
der Balkon ◇, -s *or* -e	balcony
der Bezirk, -e 📖	district
der Dachboden 📖	attic, loft
der Einwohner	inhabitant
der Gang ◇, -̈e 📖	corridor
der Kamin, -e	chimney; fireplace
der Landkreis, -e 📖	(like British) region
der Nachbar, -n	neighbour
der Rasen	lawn; grass
der Vorort, -e	suburb

IMPORTANT WORDS (f)

die Anlage 📖	layout
die Aussicht, -en 📖	view
die Decke ◇, -n	ceiling
die Gegend, -en	district, area
die Kohle	coal
die Lage, -n 📖	position, situation
die Mauer, -n 📖	(*outside*) wall
die Nachbarin	neighbour
die Telefonnummer, -n	phone number
die Terrasse, -n	patio
die Türklingel, -n	doorbell
die Umgebung	surroundings (*pl*)
die Zentralheizung	central heating

es klopft somebody's knocking at the door
es klingelt somebody's ringing the doorbell
im ersten/dritten Stock on the first/third floor
im Erdgeschoß on the ground floor, on ground level
oben upstairs; **unten** downstairs
zu Hause, daheim at home
umziehen to move (house)
einziehen to move in
sich einleben to settle down, settle in

USEFUL WORDS (m)

der Besitzer	owner
der (Fenster)laden ◇, ⁻	shutter
der *or* das (Fenster)sims, -e	window sill *or* ledge
der Hausmeister	caretaker
der Hauswirt, -e	landlord
der *or* das Kaminsims, -e	mantelpiece
der Korridor, -e	corridor
der Rauch	smoke
der Schornstein ◇, -e	chimney
der (Treppen)absatz, ⁻e	landing
der Umzug ◇, ⁻e	removal
der Wintergarten, ⁻	conservatory
der Wohnblock, -s	block of flats
der Zaun, Zäune	fence

USEFUL WORDS (f)

die Allee, -n	avenue
die Antenne, -n	aerial
die Einrichtung	furnishings (*pl*)
die Etagenwohnung, -en	flat
die Fensterscheibe, -n	window pane
die Fliese, -n	tile
die Gasse, -n	lane (*in town*)
die Hecke, -n	hedge
die Hütte ◇, -n ▢	cottage
die Jalousie, -n	venetian blind
die Kachel, -n	(wall) tile
die Kellerwohnung, -en	basement flat
die Mansarde, -n	attic
die Putzfrau, -en	cleaner
die Rumpelkammer	box room, junk room
die Stube, -n	room
die (Tür)stufe, -n	(door)step
die Verandatür, -en	French window
die (Wohn)siedlung, -en	housing estate

ESSENTIAL WORDS (m)

der Briefkasten ◇, ⁼	letterbox
der Fernsehapparat, -e *or*	
der Fernseher	television set
der Fön, -e	hair-drier
der Knopf, ⁼e	knob, button
der Kühlschrank, ⁼e	fridge
der Schalter ◇	switch
der Schrank, ⁼e	cupboard
der Topf, ⁼e	pot
der Wecker	alarm clock

ESSENTIAL WORDS (f)

die Bürste, -n	brush
die Dusche, -n	shower
die Farbe ◇, -n	paint; colour
die Gardine, -n	curtain
die Hausarbeit	housework
die Kanne, -n	jug; pot
die Lampe, -n	lamp
die Sachen (*pl*)	things
die Seife	soap
die Zahnbürste, -n	toothbrush
die Zahncreme; die Zahnpasta	toothpaste

ESSENTIAL WORDS (nt)

das Bild, -er	picture, painting
das Handtuch, ⁼er	towel
das Licht, -er	light
das Poster, -(s)	poster
das Wasser	water

die Hausarbeit machen to do the housework
duschen to have a shower
baden to have a bath
aufwecken to waken up

IMPORTANT WORDS (m)

der Abfall	rubbish, refuse
der Aschenbecher	ashtray
der Kamm, ⸚e	comb
der Rasierapparat, -e	razor
der Spiegel	mirror
der Teppich, -e	carpet
der Vorhang, ⸚e	curtain
der (Wasser)hahn ⇔, ⸚e ▭	tap

IMPORTANT WORDS (f)

die (Bade)wanne, -n	bath
die (Bett)decke ⇔, -n	blanket, cover
die Bettwäsche	bed linen
die Birne ⇔, -n	(light) bulb
die Bratpfanne, -n ▭	frying pan
die Elektrizität	electricity
die Kerze, -n ▭	candle
die Pflanze, -n	plant

IMPORTANT WORDS (nt)

das Federbett, -en	continental quilt
das Feuer	fire
das Gas	gas
das Geschirr ⇔	crockery; pots and pans
das Kissen	cushion; pillow
das Kopfkissen ▭	pillow
das Reinmachen	cleaning
das Rezept ⇔, -e	recipe
das Shampoo	shampoo
das Spülbecken	sink
das Tablett, -e	tray
das Waschbecken	washbasin

USEFUL WORDS (m)	
der Besen	broom
der Bettvorleger	bedside rug
der Deckel	lid
der Eimer	bucket
der Griff, -e	handle (*of door etc*)
der Handbesen; der Handfeger	brush
der Heizkörper	radiator
der Henkel	handle (*of jug etc*)
der Kachelofen, ⁻	tiled stove
der Kessel	kettle
der Kleiderbügel	coat hanger
der Krug, ⁻e	jug
der Mixer	(electric) blender
der Müll	rubbish, refuse
der Mülleimer	dustbin
der Papierkorb, ⁻e	waste paper basket
der Pinsel	paintbrush; brush
der Rasierpinsel	shaving brush
der Schmutz	dirt
der Schneebesen	whisk, egg beater
der Schwamm, ⁻e	sponge
der Staub	dust
der Staubsauger	vacuum cleaner, Hoover ®
der Toaströster	toaster
der Ziergegenstand, ⁻e	ornament

sein eigenes Zimmer haben to have a room of one's own
die Tür aufmachen/zumachen, die Tür öffnen/schließen
  to open/close the door
das Zimmer betreten to go into the room
putzen to clean; **abstauben** to dust
staubsaugen to hoover
bürsten to brush
waschen to wash
bügeln to iron

USEFUL WORDS (f)

die Brücke ◇, -n	(narrow) rug *or* mat
die Daunendecke, -n	eiderdown
die Fußmatte, -n	doormat
die Heizdecke, -n	electric blanket
die Kaffeemühle, -n	coffee grinder
die Leiter ◇, -n	ladder
die Matte, -n	mat
die Nackenrolle, -n	bolster
die Rasierklinge, -n	razor blade
die Röhre, -n	pipe
die Rührmaschine, -n	(electric) mixer
die Satellitenantenne, -n	satellite dish
die Steppdecke, -n	(continental) quilt
die Tapete, -n	wallpaper
die Vase, -n	vase
die Waage, -n	(set of) scales
die Wäscheschleuder, -n	spin dryer

USEFUL WORDS (nt)

das Abwaschtuch, ¨-er	dish cloth
das Brett ◇, -er	tray
das Bügelbrett, -er	ironing board *or* table
das Bügeleisen	iron
das Gemälde	painting, picture
das Geschirrtuch, ¨-er	dish cloth; tea towel
das Polster	cushion; pillow
das Rohr, -e	pipe
das Seifenpulver	soap powder
das Staubtuch, ¨-er	duster

ESSENTIAL WORDS (m)	
der Absender (Abs)	sender
der Anruf, -e	telephone call
der Bescheid, -e	information; directions (pl)
der Brief, -e	letter
der Briefkasten ◇, ¨	postbox, pillar box
der Briefträger	postman
der Fernsprecher ▭	telephone
der Groschen	10-pfennig piece
der Kugelschreiber; der Kuli, -s	ballpoint pen, biro
der Kurs, -e ▭	rate
der Name, -n	name
der Polizist, -en	policeman
der Preis, -e	price, cost
der Reisepaß, ¨sse	passport
der (Reise)scheck, -s	(traveller's) cheque
der Schalter ◇	counter
der Schilling, - or -e	schilling
der (Telefon)hörer ▭	(telephone) receiver
der Telefonist, -en	operator, telephonist
der Umschlag, ¨e	envelope
der Vorname, -n	first name, Christian name

entschuldigen Sie bitte — wo ist der nächste Briefkasten? excuse me — where is the nearest postbox?
weißt du hier Bescheid? do you know this place (well)?
wo bekomme ich Auskunft? where can I get some information?
ist es (nach Bremen) noch weit? do we have far to go (to Bremen)?
wie komme ich nach dem Bahnhof? how do I get to the station?
geradeaus straight on
die erste Straße links the first street on the left
die dritte Straße rechts the third street on the right
2 Kilometer nördlich der Stadtmitte 2 kilometres north of the town centre

ESSENTIAL WORDS (f)	
die Adresse, -n *or*	
die Anschrift, -en ⌑	address
die Ansichtskarte, -n	picture postcard
die Auskunft ◇	information; directory enquiries
die Bank ◇, -en	bank
die Bezahlung, -en	payment
die Briefkarte, -n	letter card
die Briefmarke, -n	(postage) stamp
die Einladung, -en ⌑	invitation
die (Hand)tasche, -n	(hand)bag
die Kasse ◇, -n	cash desk; check-out; till
die Mark	mark
die Münze, -n	coin
die Paketpost	parcel post
die Polizei	police
die Polizeiwache, -n	police station
die Polizistin	policewoman
die Post ◇, -en	post, mail; post office
die Postkarte, -n	postcard
die Reparatur, -en	repair, repairing
die Rückgabe, -n ⌑	return
die Sparkasse, -n	savings bank
die Taste ◇, -n ⌑	(push-)button
die Telefonistin	operator, telephonist
die Telefonzelle, -n	callbox, telephone box
die Unterschrift, -en ⌑	signature
die Vorwahlnummer, -n ◇	dialling code
die Wechselstube, -n	bureau de change

links/rechts abbiegen to turn left/right
**ich habe meine Tasche verloren — hat jemand sie
   gefunden?** I've lost my bag — has anyone found it?
beschreiben to describe
liegenlassen to leave behind; **klauen** to pinch
ein Formular ausfüllen to fill in a form
der Bank (*dat*) **Bescheid sagen** to inform the bank

ESSENTIAL WORDS (nt)

das Briefpapier	writing paper
das Formular, -e 📖	form
das Fundbüro, -s	lost property office
das Kleingeld	small change
das Päckchen	package, (*small*) parcel
das Paket, -e	parcel, package
das Portemonnaie, -s	purse
das Postamt, ̈er	post office
das Postwertzeichen 📖	postage stamp
das Problem, -e	problem
das Scheckheft, -e	cheque book
das Telefon, -e	telephone
das Telefonbuch, ̈er	telephone directory
das Verkehrsamt, ̈er	tourist information office

einen Brief schreiben to write a letter
aufgeben to send, post; **senden, schicken** to send
zur Post gehen to go to the post office
den Brief einwerfen to post the letter (*in postbox*)
ein Paket einreichen to hand in a parcel
einige Briefmarken kaufen to buy some stamps
was ist das Porto für einen Brief nach Schottland? how
  much is a letter to Scotland?
3 Briefmarken zu 80 Pfennig 3 80-pfennig stamps
ist Post für mich da? is there any mail for me?
erwarten to expect
bekommen, erhalten to get, receive
zurückschicken to send back
mit Luftpost by airmail
portofrei freepost
postlagernd poste restante

IMPORTANT WORDS (m)

der Anschluß, ⁼sse	(telephone) extension
der Fehler	fault; mistake, error
der Luftpostbrief, -e	airmail letter
der Personalausweis, -e	identity card
Postbeamte(r), -n	counter clerk
der Termin, -e	(*doctor's etc*) appointment
der Zeuge, -n ▢	witness

IMPORTANT WORDS (f)

die (Bank)note, -n	(bank)note
die Beschreibung, -en ▢	description
die Brieftasche, -n ▢	wallet
die Geldstrafe, -n ▢	fine
die Heimat, -en ▢	home (town/country *etc*)
die Leerung, -en ▢	collection (*of mail*)
die Luftpost	airmail
die Nummer, -n	number
die Postbeamtin	counter clerk
die Postgebühr, -en ▢	postage
die Scheckkarte, -n	cheque card
die Telefonnummer, -n	phone number
die Verabredung, -en	date, appointment
die Verbindung, -en	line, connection
die Währung, -en ▢	currency

ich möchte einen Scheck einlösen I'd like to cash a cheque
unterschreiben to sign
ich möchte Pfunde (in Mark) umtauschen I'd like to
change some pounds (into marks)
können Sie mir ein Pfund wechseln? can you give me
change of a pound?
wieviel Geld willst du wechseln? how much money do you
want to change?
ich habe kein Kleingeld I don't have any (small) change
bar bezahlen to pay in cash
ein Scheck über 100 Pfund a cheque for £100

IMPORTANT WORDS (nt)	
das Bargeld	cash
das Ferngespräch, -e 📖	trunk call
das Geschlecht, -er 📖	sex
das Mißverständnis, -se	misunderstanding
das Ortsgespräch, -e	local call
das Pfund Sterling	pound sterling
das R-Gespräch, -e	reverse charge call
das Telefongespräch, -e	phone call
das Telegramm, -e	telegram, cable

jdn anrufen, mit jdm telefonieren to phone or call sb
den Hörer abheben to lift the receiver
ein R-Gespräch führen to make a reverse-charge call
die Nummer nachsuchen/wählen to look up/dial the
number
können Sie mir die Vorwahlnummer sagen? can you tell
me the dialling code?
drücken to press
das Telefon läutet the phone rings
wer ist am Apparat? who's speaking?
hallo, hier ist . . . hello, this is . . .
kann ich Peter sprechen? could I speak to Peter?
bleiben Sie am Apparat hold on, please
einen Augenblick, ich verbinde Sie just a minute, I'll put
you through
eine Nachricht hinterlassen to leave a message
besetzt engaged
außer Betrieb out of order
Sie sind falsch verbunden you have the wrong number
ich habe mich verwählt I dialled the wrong number
danke für den Anruf thank you for calling
ich rufe Sie zurück I'll call you back
die Verbindung ist sehr schlecht it's a bad line
den Hörer auflegen or **einhängen** to replace the receiver

| USEFUL WORDS (m) |
---

der Einschreibebrief, -e	registered letter
der Empfänger	addressee
der Stempel	postmark

| USEFUL WORDS (f) |
---

die Belohnung, -en	reward
die Blockschrift	block capitals (*pl*)
die Drucksache, -n	printed matter
die Kaution, -en	deposit
die Postanweisung, -en	postal order
die Postleitzahl, -en	postcode
die Steuer, -n	tax

| USEFUL WORDS (nt) |
---

das Branchenverzeichnis	Yellow Pages (*pl*)
das Einwickelpapier	wrapping paper
das Konto, Konten	account
das Packpapier	brown paper, wrapping paper
das Porto	postage

sprechen Sie Englisch? do you speak English?
was heißt das auf deutsch? what's that in German?
könnten Sie das bitte wiederholen? could you repeat that please?
verstehen, kapieren to understand
wie schreibt man das? how do you spell that?
soll ich das Ihnen buchstabieren? shall I spell that for you?

Lieber Franz! Dear Frank; **Liebe Bettina!** Dear Bettina
Sehr geehrter Herr! Dear Sir; **Sehr geehrte Frau!** Dear Madam
Viele Grüße!; **Mit freundlichem** *or* **herzlichem Gruß!** Best wishes
Hochachtungsvoll Yours faithfully

ESSENTIAL WORDS (m)

der Ausweis, -e	identity card
der Polizist, -en	policeman
der Reisescheck, -s	traveller's cheque
der Scheck, -s	cheque

ESSENTIAL WORDS (f)

die Auskunft ◇, -̈e	information; particulars
die Ausweiskarte	identity card
die Bank ◇, -en	bank
die Polizei	police
die Polizistin	policewoman
die Tasche ◇, -n	bag

ESSENTIAL WORDS (nt)

das Fundbüro, -s	lost property office
das Geld, -er	money
das Portemonnaie, -s	purse

verunglücken to have an accident
jdn überfahren to run sb over
verletzt injured; **verwundet** wounded
betrunken drunk
Notruf (110) *emergency phone number*
sich versichern to be insured
Hilfe! help!; **haltet den Dieb!** stop thief!
Feuer! fire!; **Hände hoch!** hands up!
Angst haben to be afraid
stehlen to steal; **klauen** to pinch
rauben to rob
eine Bank überfallen to rob a bank
entführen, hijacken to hijack; to kidnap, abduct
verschwinden to disappear
die Polizei holen lassen to send for the police
retten to rescue; **entkommen** to escape
strafen to punish

IMPORTANT WORDS (m)

der Bandit, -en	bandit
der Demonstrant, -en	demonstrator
der Detektiv, -e	detective
der Dieb, -e ▢	thief
der Diebstahl, ⸚e	theft
der Gangster, -s	gangster
der Hijacker	hijacker
die Notdienste (*pl*)	emergency services
der Privatdetektiv, -e	private detective
der Retter	rescuer
der Revolver	gun, revolver
der Rowdy, -s *or* **-ies**	hooligan
der Sicherheitsbeamte(r), -n	security guard
der Streit, -e	argument, dispute
der Taschendieb, -e ▢	pickpocket
der Terrorist, -en	terrorist
Tote(r), -n	dead man/woman
der Überfall, ⸚e	raid; attack
der Unfall, ⸚e	accident
der Zeuge, -n ▢	witness

IMPORTANT WORDS (nt)

das Bargeld	cash, ready money
das Gericht ▷, -e	court
das Gold	gold
das Recht, -e	the law; right
das Silber	silver

---

demonstrieren to demonstrate
ein Gebäude (in die Luft) sprengen to blow up a building
erschießen to shoot (dead)
töten to kill
ermorden to murder
verhaften to arrest
ins Gefängnis kommen to go to jail
schuldig guilty; **unschuldig** innocent

IMPORTANT WORDS (f)	
die **Armee**, -n	army
die **Atomwaffe**, -n	atomic weapon
die **Bande**, -n	band, gang
die **Beschreibung**, -en ⌑	description
die **Bombe**, -n	bomb
die **Brieftasche**, -n	wallet
die **Demonstrantin**	demonstrator
die **Demonstration**, -en	demonstration
die **Diebin** ⌑	thief
die **Droge**, -n	drug
die **Erlaubnis**, -se ⌑	permission; permit
die **Gefahr**, -en ⌑	danger, risk
die **Geldstrafe**, -n ⌑	fine
die **Pflicht**, -en	duty
die **Pistole**, -n	gun, pistol
die **Rettung**, -en	rescue
die **Terroristin**	terrorist
die **Untersuchung** ⇩, -en	inquiry, investigation
die **Zeugin** ⌑	witness

USEFUL WORDS (nt)	
das **Gefängnis**, -se	prison, jail
das **Gesetz**, -e	law
das **Gewehr**, -e	gun, rifle
das **Heer**, -e	army
das **Rauschgift**, -e	drug
das **(Todes)urteil**	(death) sentence
das **Verbrechen**	crime
das **Zuchthaus**, (-häuser)	(top-security) prison

USEFUL WORDS (m)

der Beweis, -e	evidence, proof
der Brand, ⸚e	fire
der Einbrecher	burglar
der Einbruch, ⸚e	burglary, break-in
der Entführer	kidnapper; hijacker
der Feind, -e	enemy
Gefangene(r), -n	prisoner
der Gefängniswärter	prison guard
der Gerichtshof, ⸚e	law court
der Mord, -e	murder
der Mörder	murderer, killer
der Prozeß, -sse	trail, lawsuit
der Raub	robbery
der Räuber	robber
der Raubüberfall, ⸚e	robbery with violence
der (Rechts)anwalt	lawyer, barrister
der Spion, -e	spy
der Verbrecher	criminal
Verdächtige(r), -n	suspect

USEFUL WORDS (f)

die Belohnung, -en	reward
die Einbruchssicherung, -en	burglar alarm
die Festnahme, -n	arrest
die Flucht, -en	escape
die Haft	custody
die Handschellen (pl)	handcuffs
die Justiz	justice
die Kurzmeldung, -en	news flash
die Leiche, -n	corpse, body
die (Polizei)wache, -n	police station
die Regierung, -en	government
die Schuld, -en	guilt; fault
die Unschuld	innocence
die Verhaftung, -en	arrest
die Versicherungspolice	insurance policy

ESSENTIAL WORDS (m)	
der Kaugummi	chewing gum
der Stein, -e	stone, rock

ESSENTIAL WORDS (nt)	
das Aluminium	aluminium
das Benzin	petrol
das Dieselöl	diesel oil
das Gas	gas
das Glas ◇	glass
das Gummiband, ¨er	rubber band; elastic
das Leder	leather
das Öl, -e	oil
das Papier	paper

eine Baumwollbluse a cotton blouse
ein Seidenschal (*m*) a silk scarf
ein Holzstuhl (*m*) a wooden chair
ein Strohhut (*m*) a straw hat
ein Pelzmantel (*m*) a fur coat
ein Wollpullover (*m*) a woollen jumper
ein Pappkarton (*m*) a cardboard box
ein Lammfellmantel (*m*) a sheepskin coat
eine Tasche aus Leder a leather bag
die Tasche ist aus Leder the bag is made of leather
eine Vase aus Ton an earthenware vase
die Vase ist aus Ton the vase is made of earthenware
eisern, Eisen- iron
golden, Gold- gold, golden
hölzern, Holz- wooden
marmorn, Marmor- marble
silbern, Silber- silver
echt real, genuine
kostbar precious; costly, expensive

IMPORTANT WORDS (m)

der Aufkleber	sticker, label
der Denim	denim
der Fleck, -e 📖	mark, spot
der Gips	plaster; plaster of Paris
der Jeanstoff	denim
der Klebstoff	glue
der Kord	cord, corduroy
der Kunststoff	synthetic
der Polyester	polyester
der Stahl	steel
der Stoff, -e	cloth, material

IMPORTANT WORDS (f)

die Baumwolle	cotton
die Bronze	bronze
die Gebrauchsanweisung	directions for use (*pl*)
die Seide	silk

IMPORTANT WORDS (nt)

das Blei	lead
das Gold	gold
das *or* der Gummi	rubber; gum
das Holz	wood
das Material, -ien	material, cloth; material(s)
das Metall, -e	metal
das Nylon	nylon
das Petroleum	paraffin
das Plastik	plastic
das Seidenpapier	tissue paper
das Silber	silver
das Silberpapier	silver paper
das Stroh	straw
das Vinyl	vinyl
das Wildleder	suede

USEFUL WORDS *(m)*	
der **Backstein**, -e	brick
der **Beton**	concrete
der **Bindfaden**, ⁻	string
der **Draht**, ⁻e	wire
der **Faden**, ⁻	thread
der **Kalk**	lime
der **Karton**, -s	cardboard; cardboard box
der **Kautschuk**	(india)rubber (*substance*)
der **Marmor**	marble
der **Pelz**, -e	fur
der **Samt**	velvet
der **Satin**	satin
der **Schaumgummi**	foam rubber
der **Tesafilm** ®	Sellotape ®
der **Ton** ◇	clay
der **Tweed**	tweed
der **Zement**	cement
der **Ziegel(stein)**, -e	brick
der **Zustand**, ⁻e	condition

in gutem/schlechtem Zustand in good/bad condition
"vor Nässe bewahren *or* schützen" "keep dry"
etw chemisch reinigen to dry-clean sth

USEFUL WORDS (f)

die Flüßigkeit, -en	liquid
die Kohle	coal
die Leinwand ◇	canvas
die Pappe	cardboard
die Plastikfolie	clingfilm
die Schnur ◇, -̈e	cord, string
die Spitze ◇, -n	lace
die Strickwaren (*pl*)	knitwear
die Watte	cotton wool
die Wolle	wool

USEFUL WORDS (nt)

das Acryl	acrylic
das Blech	tin
das Eisen	iron
das Fell, -e	fur, coat
das Kristall	crystal
das Kupfer	copper
das Leinen	linen
das Messing	brass
das Porzellan	porcelain, china
das Schaffell	sheepskin
das Segeltuch	sailcloth, canvas
das Seil, -e	rope; cable
das Stanniolpapier	tinfoil
das Steingut	earthenware
das Styropor	polystyrene
das Wachs	wax
das Zinn	pewter; tin

ESSENTIAL + IMPORTANT WORDS (m)

der Jazz	jazz
der Musiker	musician
der Triangel	triangle
der Zuhörer	listener; (pl) audience

ESSENTIAL + IMPORTANT WORDS (f)

die Blaskapelle, -n	brass band
die Blockflöte, -n	recorder
die Flöte, -n	flute
die Geige, -n	violin, fiddle
die Gitarre, -n	guitar
die Gruppe, -n	group
die Kapelle ⟡, -n	band, orchestra
die Klarinette, -n	clarinet
die Musik	music
die Note ⟡, -n	note; (pl) music
die Oboe, -n	oboe
die Taste ⟡, -n ▭	(piano) key
die Trompete, -n	trumpet

IMPORTANT WORDS (nt)

das Akkordeon, -s	accordion
das Bügelhorn, ¨er	bugle
das Cello, -s or Celli	cello
das Horn, ¨er	horn
das Klavier, -e	piano
das Konzert ⟡, -e	concert; concerto
das (Musik)instrument, -e	(musical) instrument
das Orchester	orchestra; band
das Saxophon, -e	saxophone
das Schlagzeug	drums (pl)
das Xylophon, -e	xylophone

Klavier/Gitarre spielen to play the piano/the guitar
die Schlagermusik pop music; **die klassische Musik**
classical music; **die Blasmusik** brass band music

USEFUL WORDS (m)

der Akkord	chord
der Chor, ̈-e	choir; chorus
der Dirigent, -en	conductor
der Dudelsack	bagpipes (*pl*)
der Flügel ◇	grand piano
der Kontrabaß, (-bässe)	double bass
der Solist, -en	soloist
der Taktstock	(conductor's) baton
der Ton ◇, ̈-e	note

USEFUL WORDS (f)

die Harfe, -n	harp
die Konzerthalle, -n	concert hall
die Mundharmonika	mouth organ, harmonica
die Musikkapelle, -n	band (*circus, military etc*)
die Oper, -n	opera; opera house
die Orgel, -n	organ
die Posaune, -n	trombone
die Querflöte, -n	flute
die Saite, -n	string
die Solistin	soloist
die Tastatur	keyboard
die Tonart, -en	(musical) key
die (große) Trommel	(big, bass) drum
die Violine	violin
die Ziehharmonika, -s	concertina; accordion

USEFUL WORDS (nt)

die Becken (*pl*)	cymbals
das Fagott, -s *or* -e	bassoon
das Jagdhorn, ̈-er	bugle; hunting horn
das Opernhaus, (-häuser)	opera house
das Streichorchester	string orchestra
das Tamburin, -e	tambourine
das Violoncello, -s *or* -celli	violoncello
das Waldhorn, ̈-er	French horn

CARDINAL NUMBERS

nought	0	null
one	1	eins
two	2	zwei
three	3	drei
four	4	vier
five	5	fünf
six	6	sechs
seven	7	sieben
eight	8	acht
nine	9	neun
ten	10	zehn
eleven	11	elf
twelve	12	zwölf
thirteen	13	dreizehn
fourteen	14	vierzehn
fifteen	15	fünfzehn
sixteen	16	sechzehn
seventeen	17	siebzehn
eighteen	18	achtzehn
nineteen	19	neunzehn
twenty	20	zwanzig
twenty-one	21	einundzwanzig
twenty-two	22	zweiundzwanzig
twenty-three	23	dreiundzwanzig
thirty	30	dreißig
thirty-one	31	einunddreißig
thirty-two	32	zweiunddreißig
forty	40	vierzig
fifty	50	fünfzig
sixty	60	sechzig
seventy	70	siebzig
eighty	80	achtzig
ninety	90	neunzig
ninety-nine	99	neunundneunzig
a (or one) hundred	100	hundert

CARDINAL NUMBERS (cont)

a hundred and one	**101**	hunderteins
a hundred and two	**102**	hundertzwei
a hundred and ten	**110**	hundertzehn
a hundred and		hundertzweiund-
eighty-two	**182**	achtzig
two hundred	**200**	zweihundert
two hundred and one	**201**	zweihunderteins
two hundred and two	**202**	zweihundertzwei
three hundred	**300**	dreihundert
four hundred	**400**	vierhundert
five hundred	**500**	fünfhundert
six hundred	**600**	sechshundert
seven hundred	**700**	siebenhundert
eight hundred	**800**	achthundert
nine hundred	**900**	neunhundert
a (*or* one) thousand	**1000**	(ein)tausend
a thousand and one	**1001**	tausendeins
a thousand and two	**1002**	tausendzwei
two thousand	**2000**	zweitausend
ten thousand	**10 000**	zehntausend
a (*or* one) hundred		
thousand	**100 000**	hunderttausend
a (*or* one) million	**1 000 000**	eine Million
two million	**2 000 000**	zwei Millionen

1979   neunzehnhundertneunundsiebzig *or*
tausendneunhundertneunundsiebzig

gerade/ungerade Zahlen even/odd numbers
50 Prozent 50 per cent

ORDINAL NUMBERS

These can be masculine, feminine or neuter, and take the appropriate endings.

first	der Erste
second	der Zweite
third	der Dritte
fourth	der Vierte
fifth	der Fünfte
sixth	der Sechste
seventh	der Siebente
eighth	der Achte
ninth	der Neunte
tenth	der Zehnte
eleventh	der Elfte
twelfth	der Zwölfte
thirteenth	der Dreizehnte
fourteenth	der Vierzehnte
fifteenth	der Fünfzehnte
sixteenth	der Sechzehnte
seventeenth	der Siebzehnte
eighteenth	der Achtzehnte
nineteenth	der Neunzehnte
twentieth	der Zwanzigste
twenty-first	der Einundzwanzigste
twenty-second	der Zweiundzwanzigste
thirtieth	der Dreißigste
thirty-first	der Einunddreißigste
fortieth	der Vierzigste
fiftieth	der Fünfzigste
sixtieth	der Sechzigste
seventieth	der Siebzigste
eightieth	der Achtzigste
ninetieth	der Neunzigste
hundredth	der Hunderste
hundred and first	der Hunderterste
hundred and tenth	der Hundertzehnte

ORDINAL NUMBERS (cont)

two hundredth	der Zweihundertste
three hundredth	der Dreihundertste
four hundredth	der Vierhundertste
five hundredth	der Fünfhundertste
six hundredth	der Sechshundertste
seven hundredth	der Siebenhundertste
eight hundredth	der Achthundertste
nine hundredth	der Neunhundertste
thousandth	der Tausendste
two thousandth	der Zweitausendste
millionth	der Million(s)te
two millionth	der Zweimillion(s)te

zum zigsten Male for the umpteenth time
ein Millionär a millionaire

FRACTIONS

a half	halb, die Hälfte
one and half kilos	eineinhalb Kilos, anderthalb Kilos
two and a half kilos	zweieinhalb Kilos
a third	ein Drittel (*nt*)
two thirds	zwei Drittel
a quarter	ein Viertel (*nt*)
three quarters	drei Viertel
a sixth	ein Sechstel (*nt*)
five and five sixths	fünf und fünfsechstel
an eighth	ein Achtel (*nt*)
a twelfth	ein Zwölftel (*nt*)
a twentieth	ein Zwanzigstel (*nt*)
a hundredth	ein Hundertstel (*nt*)
a thousandth	ein Tausendstel (*nt*)
a millionth	ein Millionstel (*nt*)

(0, 4) Null Komma vier (0.4) nought point four
die Flasche war dreiviertel leer the bottle was three-quarters empty

NUMBERS and QUANTITIES

der Becher ⇨ (Joghurt)	pot (of yogurt)
ein bißchen	a little (bit of)
die Büchse ⇨	tin, can
der *or* das Deziliter	decilitre
das Dutzend	dozen
Dutzende von etwas	dozens of
etwas	a little (bit of)
das Faß	barrel
die Flasche (Wein)	bottle (of wine)
das Glas ⇨ (Milch)	glass (of milk)
das Glas ⇨ Marmelade	jar *or* pot of jam
eine Halbe	a half (litre of beer etc)
ein halbes Dutzend/ Pfund	half-a-dozen/-pound, a half dozen/pound
ein halbes Kilo/Liter	half a kilo/litre
die Handvoll (Münzen)	handful (of coins)
der Haufen	heap, pile
ein Haufen	heaps of
Hunderte von	hundreds of
hundert Gramm Käse	a hundred grammes of cheese
die Kanne (Kaffee)	pot (of coffee)
das Kilo(gramm)	kilo(gramme)
ein Kleines	a half pint (*of beer etc*)
das Knäuel Wolle, das Wollknäuel	ball of wool
das Liter	litre
die Menge	crowd; heaps of
das Meter (Stoff)	metre (of cloth)
das Paar ⇨ (Schuhe)	pair (of shoes)
das Päckchen	packet
die Packung Keks/ Zigaretten	packet of biscuits/ cigarettes
das Pfund (Kartoffeln)	pound (of potatoes)
die Portion (Eis)	portion *or* helping (of ice cream)
der Riegel Seife/ Schokolade	cake *or* bar of soap/ chocolate

NUMBERS and QUANTITIES (cont)	
die **Schachtel**	box; packet (*of cigarettes*)
die **Schar**	group, band
die **Scheibe (Brot)**	slice (of bread)
die **Schüssel**	bowl, dish
der **Stapel**	pile
das **Stück ▷ Zucker**	lump of sugar
das **Stück ▷ Kuchen**	piece *or* slice of cake
das **Stück ▷ Papier**	bit *or* piece of paper
die **Tafel ▷ Schokolade**	bar of chocolate
die **Tasse(voll)**	cup(ful)
Tausende von	thousands of
der **Teller**	plate
das **Viertel(pfund)**	quarter(-pound)
ein **wenig**	a little (bit) of
der **Würfel Zucker**	lump of sugar
der **Würfel Margarine**	half a pound of margarine (*in cube shape*)

dem Dutzend/dem Hundert/dem Tausend nach by the
  dozen/the hundred/the thousand
für das Dutzend/das Hundert/das Tausend per dozen/
  hundred/thousand, (for) a dozen/a hundred/a thousand

ESSENTIAL WORDS (m)

der Artikel	article
der Ohrring, -e	earring
der Rasierapparat, -e 🗀	razor
der Ring, -e	ring
der Schlüsselring	key-ring
der Schmuck	jewellery

ESSENTIAL WORDS (f)

die Armbanduhr, -en	(wrist) watch
die Bürste, -n	brush
die Halskette, -n	necklace
die Kette, -n	chain
die Rasiercreme	shaving cream
die Sache, -n	thing
die Schönheit	beauty
die Seife	soap
die Zahnbürste, -n	toothbrush
die Zahnpasta	toothpaste

ESSENTIAL + IMPORTANT WORDS (nt)

das Armband, ⁻er	bracelet
das Deodorant(spray), -s/(-s)	deodorant
das Gold	gold
das Haarwaschmittel 🗀	shampoo
das Handtuch, ⁻er	towel
das Juwel, -en	jewel; (pl) jewels, jewellery
das Make-up	foundation; make-up
das Parfüm, -s or -e	perfume, scent
das Rasierwasser	after-shave
das Shampoo, -s	shampoo
das Silber	silver
das Taschengeld	pocket money
das Toilettenwasser	toilet water

baden to have a bath; **duschen** to have a shower

IMPORTANT WORDS (m)	
der Ehering, -e	wedding ring
der Gesichtspuder	face powder
der Kamm, ⸚e	comb
der Schönheitssalon	beauty salon
der Spiegel	mirror

IMPORTANT WORDS (f)	
die Gesichtscreme	face cream
die Kosmetik	cosmetics (*pl*), make-up
die Perle, -n	pearl; bead
die Perlenkette, -n	beads, string of beads

USEFUL WORDS (m)	
der Anhänger ⸎	pendant
der Edelstein, -e	gem, precious stone
der Lidschatten	eyeshadow
der Lippenstift, -e	lipstick
der Lockenwickler	curler, roller
der Manschettenknopf, ⸚e	cufflink
der Nagellack	nail varnish, nail polish
der Nagellackentferner	nail varnish remover
der Schwamm, ⸚e	sponge
der Trauring, -e	wedding ring
der Waschbeutel	toilet bag
der Waschlappen	face flannel

USEFUL WORDS (f)	
die Brosche, -n	brooch
die Frisur, -en	hairstyle
die Krawattennadel, -n	tie-pin
die Perücke, -n	wig
die Puderdose, -n	(powder) compact
die Schminke, -n	make-up
die Wimperntusche	mascara

sich rasieren to shave; **kämmen** to comb; **bürsten** to brush

---

ESSENTIAL WORDS (m)

der Baum, Bäume	tree
der Blumentopf, ⁻e	flower pot
der Garten, ⁻	garden
der Gärtner	gardener
der Gemüsegarten, ⁻	vegetable garden
der Grund ⟡	ground
der Obstgarten, ⁻	orchard
der Regen	rain
der Sonnenschein	sunshine
der Stein, -e	stone, rock

ESSENTIAL WORDS (f)

die Biene, -n	bee
die Blume, -n	flower
die Erde, -n	earth, soil
die (Garten)bank ⟡, ⁻e	(garden) seat *or* bench
die Gartentür, -en	garden gate
die Rose, -n	rose
die Sonne	sun
die Wespe, -n	wasp

ESSENTIAL WORDS (nt)

das Blatt, ⁻er	leaf
das Gärtnern	gardening
das Gemüse	vegetable(s)
das Gras	grass

Blumen pflanzen to plant flowers
die Pflanzen wachsen the plants grow
gießen to water
pflücken to pick
**ein Strauß Rosen/Veilchen, ein Rosenstrauß/
  Veilchenstrauß** a bunch of roses/violets

IMPORTANT WORDS (m)	
der Boden ◊, ⸚	ground, soil
der Busch, ⸚e	bush, shrub
der Krokus, - *or* -se	crocus
der Pfad, -e	path
der Rasen	lawn; turf
der Schatten	shadow; shade
der Stamm, ⸚e	trunk
der Steingarten, ⸚	rockery, rock garden
der Weg ◊, -e	path
der Wurm, ⸚er	worm

IMPORTANT WORDS (f)	
die Chrysantheme, -n	chrysanthemum
die Dahlie, -n	dahlia
die Hütte ◊, -n ▫	hut, shed
die Hyazinthe, -n	hyacinth
die Lilie, -n	lily
die Orchidee, -n	orchid
die Pflanze, -n	plant
die Sonnenblume, -n	sunflower
die Tulpe, -n	tulip

IMPORTANT WORDS (nt)	
das Gartenhaus, (-häuser)	summerhouse
das Laub(werk)	leaves (*pl*), foliage
das Unkraut	weed(s)
das Werkzeug, -e	tool

den Garten umgraben to dig the garden
den Rasen mähen to mow the lawn
im Schatten eines Baumes in the shade of a tree
im Schatten bleiben to stay in the shade
allerlei Pflanzen all kinds of plants
hier duftet es (gut) what a nice smell there is here

PLANTS and GARDENS

USEFUL WORDS (m)	
der Ast, ∵e	branch
der Baumstamm, ∵e	tree trunk
der Blumenstrauß, (-sträuße)	bunch or bouquet of flowers
der Dorn, -en	thorn
der Duft, ∵e	perfume, scent
der Efeu	ivy
der Flieder	lilac
der Goldlack	wallflower
der Halm, -e	stalk, blade
der Löwenzahn	dandelion
der Mohn, -e	poppy
der Rasenmäher	lawnmower
der Rosenstock, ∵e	rose bush
der Samen	seed(s)
der Schlauch, Schläuche	garden hose
der Schmetterling, -e	butterfly
der Schubkarren	wheelbarrow
der Stachel, -n	thorn
der Stengel; der Stiel, -e	stalk, stem
der Strauch, Sträucher	shrub
der Strauß ◇, Sträuße	bunch or bouquet (of flowers)
der Tau ◇	dew
der Weiher	pond
der Wintergarten, ∵	conservatory
der Zaun, Zäune	fence
der Zweig, -e	branch

Unkraut jäten to do the weeding
die Hecke schneiden to cut the hedge
die Blätter zusammenharken to rake up the leaves
umzäunt fenced in
sonnig sunny; **schattig** shady

USEFUL WORDS (f)

die Beere, -n	berry
die Blüte	blossom
die Butterblume, -n	buttercup
die Gartenwicke	sweet pea
die Gießkanne, -n	watering can
die Hacke, -n	hoe
die Harke, -n	rake
die Hecke, -n	hedge
die Heckenschere, -n	hedge-cutters, garden shears
die Hortensie	hydrangea
die Knospe, -n	bud
die Leiter ♢, -n	ladder
die Margerite, -n	daisy
die Narzisse, -n	narcissus, daffodil
die Nelke, -n	carnation
die Osterglocke, -n	daffodil
die Pforte, -n	(garden) gate
die Primel, -n	primrose
die Rabatte, -n	border, flower bed
die Walze, -n	roller
die Wurzel, -n	root

USEFUL WORDS (nt)

das Blumenbeet, -e	flowerbed
das Gänseblümchen	daisy
das Geißblatt	honeysuckle
das Gewächshaus, (-häuser)	greenhouse
das Maiglöckchen	lily of the valley
das Schneeglöckchen	snowdrop
das Stiefmütterchen	pansy
das Veilchen	violet
das Vergißmeinnicht, -e	forget-me-not

ESSENTIAL WORDS (m)

der Ausflug, ⸚e	trip, outing
der Badeanzug, ⸚e	swimming *or* bathing costume
der Bikini, -s	bikini
der Dampfer	steamer
der Fahrgast, ⸚e ▭	passenger
der Fisch, -e	fish
der Fischer	fisherman
der Hafen, ⸚	port, harbour
der Passagier, -e	passenger
der Schwimmer	swimmer
der Seehafen, ⸚	seaport
der Seemann, (-leute)	sailor, seaman
der Sonnenschein	sunshine
der Spaziergang, ⸚e	walk
der Stein, -e	stone, rock
der Strand, ⸚e	shore, beach
der Urlauber	holiday-maker

ESSENTIAL WORDS (f)

die Ansichtskarte, -n	postcard
die Badehose, -n	swimming *or* bathing trunks
die Fähre, -n ▭	ferry
die Hafenstadt, ⸚e	port
die Insel, -n	island
die Mannschaft ◇, -en	crew
die Schwimmerin	swimmer
die See ◇, -n	sea
die Seekrankheit	seasickness
die Seeluft	sea air
die Sonne	sun
die Sonnenbrille, -n	(pair of) sunglasses
die Sonnencreme	sun(-tan) cream
die Überfahrt, -en	crossing
die Urlauberin	holiday-maker

ESSENTIAL WORDS (nt)	
das Ausland	abroad
das Bad ◊, ¨er	bathe (*in sea*), swim
das Badetuch, ¨er	(bath) towel
das Boot, -e	boat
das Fischerboot, -e	fishing boat
das Meer, -e	ocean, sea
das Picknick, -e *or* -s	picnic
das Ruder	oar; rudder
das Schiff, -e	ship, vessel
das Schwimmen	swimming
das Wasser	water

IMPORTANT WORDS (m)	
der Anker	anchor
Badende(r), -n	bather, swimmer
der Bord ◊, -e	board
der Horizont	horizon
der (Meeres)boden	bottom (of the sea)
der Ozean, -e	ocean
der Prospekt, -e	leaflet, brochure
der Rettungsring, -e	lifebelt
der Rettungsschwimmer	lifeguard
der Sand, -e	sand
der Segler	sailor, yachtsman

zwei Wochen Urlaub two weeks' holiday
am Meer at the seaside
ans Meer *or* **an die See fahren** to go to the seaside
es ist Flut/Ebbe the tide is in/out
schwimmen gehen to go for a swim
sich ausruhen to have a rest
sich sonnen to sunbathe
am Strand on the beach
eine Sonnenbrille tragen to wear sunglasses
braun werden to get a tan
einen Sonnenstich bekommen to get sunstroke

IMPORTANT WORDS (f)	
die Flagge, -n	flag
die Küste, -n	coast, shore; seaside
die Luftmatratze, -n	lilo, airbed
die Seglerin	sailor, yachtsman
die Vergnügungsfahrt, -en	pleasure cruise

IMPORTANT WORDS (nt)	
das Reisebüro, -s	travel agent's
das Segel	sail
das Segeln	sailing
das Teleskop, -e	telescope
das Ufer ⬦▢	shore (*lake*); bank (*river*)

USEFUL WORDS (m)	
der Eimer	bucket
der Jachthafen, ⸚	marina
der Kahn, ⸚e	(*small*) boat
der Kai, -e *or* -s	quay, quayside
der Kieselstein, -e	pebble
der Krebs, -e	crab
der Leuchtturm, ⸚e	lighthouse
der Liegestuhl, ⸚e	deckchair
der Mast, -e(n)	mast
der Matrose, -n	sailor
der Pier	pier
der Schaum	foam
der Schiffbruch, ⸚e	shipwreck
der Schornstein ⬦, -e	funnel
der (See)tang, -e	seaweed
der Sonnenstich	sunstroke
der Spaten	spade

USEFUL WORDS (f)

die Boje, -n	buoy
die Bucht, -en	bay
die Ebbe, -n	low tide
die Fahne, -n	flag
die Flotte, -n	navy, fleet
die Flut ⇨, -en	high tide
die Jacht, -en	yacht
die Klippe, -n	cliff
die Kreuzfahrt, -en	cruise
die Last, -en	load, cargo
die Möwe, -n	seagull
die Mündung, -en	mouth (of river)
die Muschel(schale), -n/(-n)	shell
die Sandburg, -en	sandcastle
die (Schiffs)ladung, -en	cargo
die Schwimmweste, -n	life jacket
die (Sonnen)bräune	(sun)tan
die Strömung, -en	current
die Welle, -n	wave

USEFUL WORDS (nt)

das Deck, -s or **-e**	deck (of ship)
das Fahrgeld, -er	fare
das Floß, ̈-e	raft
das Steuer ⇨	helm, tiller
das Tretboot, -e	pedal-boat, pedalo

eine Bootsfahrt machen to go on a boat trip
an Bord gehen to go on board
ruhig calm; **stürmisch** stormy; **bewegt** choppy
seekrank werden to get seasick
untergehen to go under
ertrinken to drown

ESSENTIAL WORDS (m)

der Artikel	article
der Bäcker	baker
der Einkauf, (-käufe)	shopping; purchase
der Fahrstuhl, ⁼e	lift
der Geschäftsmann, (-leute)	businessman
der Groschen	10-pfennig piece
der Kiosk, -e	kiosk
der Kunde, -n ▢	customer, client
der Laden ⬦, ⁼	shop
der Lift, -e or -s	lift
der Markt, ⁼e	market
der Pfennig, -e	pfennig
der Preis, -e	price
der Schalter ⬦	counter (post office, bank etc)
der Scheck, -s	cheque
der Schein, -e	(bank)note
der Schilling, - or -e	schilling
der Schuhmacher	shoemaker, shoe repairer
der Sommerschlußverkauf ▢	summer sale
der Stock, Stockwerke	floor
der Supermarkt, ⁼e	supermarket

einkaufen gehen to go shopping
Einkäufe machen to do the shopping
Schlange stehen to queue up
kaufen to buy; verkaufen to sell
jdn bedienen, jdm dienen to serve sb
kann ich Ihnen behilflich sein? can I help you?
was darf es sein, bitte? what would you like?
ich möchte ... I'd like ...
ich brauche ... I need ...
etw bezahlen to pay for sth
ich zahle, aber ... I'll pay but ...
etwas stimmt nicht there's something wrong somewhere
ich möchte mich nur mal umsehen I'm just looking

ESSENTIAL WORDS (f)
---

die Apotheke, -n	chemist's, pharmacy
die Bäckerei, -en	bakery, baker's (shop)
die Bank ◇, -en	bank
die Bibliothek, -en	library
die Buchhandlung, -en	bookshop, bookseller's
die Drogerie, -n	(retail) chemist's
die Etage, -n	floor
die Farbe ◇, -n	colour
die Geschäftszeit, -en	business hours
die Größe ◇, -n	size
die Handlung ◇, -en	shop
die Kasse ◇, -n	till; cash desk, checkout
die Konditorei, -en	cake shop
die Kundin ▭	customer, client
die Liste, -n	list
die Mark	mark (*money*)
die Metzgerei, -en	butcher's (shop)
die Öffnungszeit, -en	opening time
die Post ◇, -en	post office
die Rechnung, -en	bill
die Schachtel, -n	box
die Schuhgröße, -n	shoe size
die Selbstbedienung (SB) ▭	self-service
die Sparkasse, -n	savings bank
die Tierhandlung, -en	pet shop
die Tüte, -n	bag

erhältlich available; **ausverkauft** sold out
beim Bäcker/Fleischer at the baker's/butcher's
anbieten to offer
etw probieren to try sth (*taste, sample*)
etw anprobieren to try sth on
das gefällt mir I like that
wählen to choose
wiegen to weigh

ESSENTIAL WORDS (nt)

das Büro, -s	office
das Café, -s	café
das Einkaufen	shopping
das Erdgeschoß, -sse	ground level, ground floor
das Geld	money
das Geschäft ◊, -e	shop; trade, business; deal
das Geschenk, -e	present, gift
das Kaufhaus, (-häuser)	department store
das Kleingeld	small change
das Portemonnaie, -s	purse
das Postamt, ̈-er	post office
das Restaurant, -s	restaurant
das Schuhgeschäft, -e	shoe shop
das Sonderangebot, -e 📖	bargain (offer), special offer
das Souvenir, -s	souvenir
das Warenhaus, (-häuser)	department store, general store
das Wirtshaus, (-häuser)	pub, inn

was kostet es? what does it cost?
was macht das? what does that come to?
ich habe 15 Mark dafür bezahlt I paid 15 marks for it
einen Scheck ausstellen to write out a cheque
bar bezahlen to pay cash
Geld für Pralinen ausgeben to spend money on chocolates
zu teuer too dear
ganz billig quite cheap
kostenlos free, free of charge
umsonst for nothing
preiswert good value
ein preiswertes Angebot a bargain
das habe ich günstig bekommen I got it at a good price
das ist aber günstig! what a bargain!

IMPORTANT WORDS (*m*)
---

der Apotheker	(dispensing) chemist
der Aufzug, ‑̈e 📖	lift
der Ausverkauf	sale
die Betriebsferien (*pl*)	holidays (*of a business*)
der Buchhändler	bookseller
der Drogist, ‑en	retail chemist
der Einkaufskorb, (‑körbe)	shopping basket
der Einkaufswagen	shopping trolley
der Fischhändler	fishmonger
der Fleischer	butcher
der Friseur, ‑e	hairdresser
der Händler	dealer
der Herrenfriseur, ‑e	barber, men's hairdresser
der Juwelier	jeweller
der Kassenzettel	receipt
der Kaufmann, (‑leute) 📖	merchant
der Metzger	butcher
der Obst- und Gemüsehändler	greengrocer
der Obsthändler	fruiterer
der Ruhetag	(early) closing day
der Schallplattenhändler	record dealer
der Schlußverkauf, (‑käufe)	(end-of-season) sale
der Sonderpreis, ‑e 📖	special price
der Tabakladen, ‑̈	tobacconist's (shop)
der Umtausch, ‑̈e	exchange (*of goods*)
der Verkauf, ‑̈e	sale
der Verkäufer	salesman, shop assistant
der Zeitungshändler	newsagent

GmbH Ltd
AG plc

IMPORTANT WORDS (f)

die Abteilung, -en	department
die Anprobe ▢	trying on
die Auswahl (an + dat)	choice (of)
die Brieftasche, -n	wallet
die Firma, Firmen	firm, company
die Fleischerei, -en	butcher's (shop)
die Friseuse, -n	hairdresser
die Gaststätte, -n	restaurant; pub
die Gesellschaft, -en	company; society
die Kneipe, -n	pub
die Münzwäscherei	launderette
die Packung, -en	packet, box
die Parfümerie, -n	perfume counter or shop
die Quittung, -en	receipt
die Schaufensterpuppe, -n	dummy, model
die Schlange ◇, -n ▢	queue
die Schreibwarenhandlung, -en	stationer's
die Theke, -n	counter (in café, bar etc)
die Verkäuferin	salesgirl, shop assistant
die Waren (pl)	goods, wares

IMPORTANT WORDS (nt)

das Einkaufszentrum	shopping centre
das Juweliergeschäft, -e	jeweller's (shop)
das Milchgeschäft, -e	dairy
das Obergeschoß	upper floor
das Produkt, -e	product; (pl) produce
das Reisebüro, -s	travel agent's
das Schaufenster	shop window
das Untergeschoß	basement

einen Schaufensterbummel machen to go window-shopping

USEFUL WORDS (m)

der Buchmacher	bookmaker, "bookie"
der Eisenwarenhändler	ironmonger
der (Flick)schuster	cobbler, shoe repairer
der Gelegenheitskauf, (-käufe)	bargain
der Grundstücksmakler	estate agent
der Gutschein, -e	voucher
der Handel	trade, business
der Ladentisch, -e	counter (*in shop*)
der Lebensmittelhändler	grocer
der Optiker	optician
der Uhrmacher	watchmaker
der Waschsalon, -s	launderette

USEFUL WORDS (f)

die Bausparkasse, -n	building society
die Besorgung, -en	errand; purchase
die Bücherei, -en	library
die Bude, -n	stall
die Eisenwarenhandlung, -en	ironmonger's, hardware shop
die Filiale, -n	branch
die Garantie, -n	guarantee
die Kragenweite	collar size
die Reinigung	cleaner's
die Rolltreppe, -n	escalator
die Versicherungsgesell-schaft, -̈e	insurance company
die Videothek, -en	video shop
die Wäscherei, -en	laundry, cleaner's

USEFUL WORDS (nt)

das Erzeugnis, -se	product; produce
das Lebensmittelgeschäft, -e	grocer's, general food store
das Parterre, -s	ground floor
das Wechselgeld	change

ESSENTIAL WORDS (m)	
der Ball, ⁼e	ball
der Fußball, ⁼e	football
der Fußballfan, -s	football supporter
der Fußballspieler	footballer
der Läufer	runner
der Paß ◇, ⁼sse	pass
der Radsport	cycling
der Rollschuh, -e	roller skate
der Schlittschuh, -e	ice skate
der Spieler	player
der Sport, -e	sport, game
der Sportplatz, ⁼e	sports ground, playing field
der Wintersport	winter sport(s)

ESSENTIAL WORDS (nt)	
das Angeln	fishing, angling
das Endspiel, -e	final(s)
das Fitneßzentrum, -tren	health club
das Freibad, ⁼er	open-air swimming pool
das Hallenbad, ⁼er	indoor swimming pool
das Hockey	hockey
das Kricket	cricket
das Laufen	running
das Radfahren	cycling
das Reiten	horse-riding
das Rudern	rowing
das Rugby	rugby
das Schlittschuhlaufen	(ice) skating
das Schwimmbad, ⁼er	swimming baths
das Schwimmen	swimming
das Spiel ◇, -e	play; game, match
das Squash	squash
das Station, -ien	stadium
das Tennis	tennis
das Turnen ◇	gymnastics

IMPORTANT WORDS (m)

der Basketball	basketball
der Fußballplatz, ⸚e	football pitch
der Golfplatz, ⸚e	golf course
der Golfschläger	golf club (*stick*)
der Netzball	netball
der Platz ⟡, ⸚e	ground, playing field
der Pokal, -e	cup
der Profi, -s	pro
der Schläger	racket/bat/club *etc*
der Ski, -er	ski
der Teilnehmer ▭	participant
der Tennisplatz, ⸚e	tennis court
der Volleyball	volleyball
der Zuschauer ⟡ ▭	spectator

ESSENTIAL + IMPORTANT WORDS (f)

die Angelrute, -n	fishing rod
die Bundesliga ▭	football league
die Fußballelf, -en	football team
die Halbzeit	half (*of match*); half-time
die Leichtathletik	athletics
die Mannschaft ⟡, -en	team
die Rennbahn, -en	racecourse, track
die Spielerin	player
die Spielhälfte, -n	half (*of match*)
die Turnhalle, -n	gym(nasium)
die Weltmeisterschaft	world championship(s)

---

treibst du gern Sport? do you like sports?
spielen to play; **laufen** to run
werfen to throw; **springen** to jump
trainieren to train; **joggen** to go jogging
üben to practise; **trimmen** to do exercises
gewinnen to win; **verlieren** to lose
unentschieden enden to end in a draw

IMPORTANT WORDS (nt)

das Billard	billiards
das Boxen	boxing
das Ergebnis, -se 🕮	result
das Golf(spiel)	golf
das Jogging	jogging
das Netz, -en	net
das Pferderennen	horse racing; horse-race
das Rennen	racing, race meeting
das Schießen	shooting
das Segeln	sailing
das Skifahren; das Skilaufen	skiing
das Tauchen	(underwater) diving
das Tischtennis	table tennis
das Tor ◇, -e	goal
das Wasserball 🕮	water polo
das Ziel, -e	goal, aim; finish, finishing post

USEFUL WORDS (nt)

das Bergsteigen	mountaineering
das Bogenschießen	archery
das Bowls-Spiel	bowls
das gemischte Doppel	mixed doubles
das Drachenfliegen	hang-gliding
das Fechten	fencing
das Getümmel	scrum(mage)
das Jagen	hunting; shooting
das Klettern	climbing, mountaineering
die Olympischen Spiele (pl)	Olympic Games
das Ringen	wrestling
das Tauziehen	tug-of-war
das Training	training
das Turnier, -e	tournament
das Wasserski	water-skiing
das Wellenreiterbrett, -er	surfboard

USEFUL WORDS (m)	
der Bergsteiger	mountaineer
der Federball	badminton; shuttlecock
der Gegner	opponent
der Hochsprung, ⸚e	high jump
der Kampf, ⸚e	fight; contest
der Meister	champion
der Rodel	toboggan
der Satz ◇, ⸚e	set (*tennis*)
der Schiedsrichter	referee; umpire
der Schlitten	sledge, sleigh
der Sieger	winner
der Stoß, ⸚e	kick; push, thrust
der Titelverteidiger	title-holder
der Torwart, -e	goalkeeper
der Trainer	trainer, coach; manager
die Turnschuhe (*pl*)	tennis *or* gym shoes
Unparteiische(r), -n	umpire; referee
der Weitsprung, ⸚e	long jump
der (Welt)rekord, -e	(world) record
der Wettbewerb, -e	competition
der Wettkampf, ⸚e	match, contest

USEFUL WORDS (f)	
die (Aschen)bahn, -en	(cinder) track
die Eisbahn, -en	ice rink, skating rink
die Kegelbahn, -en	bowling alley; skittle alley
die Meisterschaft, -en	championship
die Partie	game, match
die Punktzahl, -en	score
die Runde, -n	lap, round
die Siegerin	winner
die Stoppuhr, -en	stopwatch
die (Tabellen)spitze, -n	lead (*in league etc*)
die Tribüne ◇, -n	stand
die Versammlung, -en	meeting

ESSENTIAL WORDS (m)

der Ausgang, ⁻e	exit, way out
der Eingang, ⁻e	entrance, way in
der Eintritt, -e 📖	entrance (*of actor onto stage*)
der Film, -e	film
der Kinobesucher	cinema-goer
der Quatsch	rubbish
der Theaterbesucher	theatre-goer
die Zuhörer (*pl*)	audience (*listeners*)

ESSENTIAL WORDS (f)

die Freizeit	free *or* spare time
die Handlung ◊, -en	plot, action
die Kasse ◊, -n	box office, ticket office
die Musik	music
die Reservierung, -en	booking
die (Theater)karte ◊, -n	(theatre) ticket
die (Theater)kasse ◊, -n	box office
die Vorstellung, -en	performance, show

ESSENTIAL WORDS (nt)

das Kino, -s	cinema
das Konzert ◊, -e	concert
das Spiel ◊	acting; play
das Theater	theatre
das (Theater)stück ◊, -e	play

---

ich gehe gern ins Kino/ins Theater I like going to the cinema/the theatre
an der Vorverkaufkasse at the booking office
"ausverkauft" "sold out"
mein Lieblingsfilmstar my favourite film star
ein Film mit Untertiteln a film with subtitles
spannend exciting; **langweilig** boring
(kaum) sehenswert (hardly) worth seeing

IMPORTANT WORDS (m)

der Applaus, -e	applause
der Balkon ⃗, -s *or* -e	(dress) circle
der Bühneneingang	stage door
der Dramatiker	dramatist, playwright
der (Film)star ⃗, -s	(film) star
der Komiker	comedian
der Konzertsaal, (-säle)	concert hall
der Krieg, -e	war
der Krimi	thriller
der Kritiker	critic
der Rang	circle (*in theatre*)
der Saal, Säle	hall; room
der Schauspieler	actor
der (Sitz)platz, ⃛e	seat
der Spaß ⃗	fun
der Spielplan, ⃛e	programme
der Text, -e	script
der Theaterzettel	programme (*leaflet*)
der Titel	title
der Untertitel	subtitle
der Vorhang, ⃛e ⊡	curtain
der Western, -s	western
die Zuschauer (*pl*) ⃗ ⊡	audience (*viewers*)
der erste Rang	dress circle
der zweite Rang	upper circle

die Bühne betreten to step onto the stage
meine Damen und Herren! ladies and gentlemen!
ein Stück geben to put on a play
mit X und Y in den Hauptrollen with X and Y in the main parts
klatschen to clap

IMPORTANT WORDS (f)

die Aufführung, -en	performance
die Bühne, -n	stage, platform
die Ermäßigung, -en	reduction
die Figur ◊, -en	character
die Garderobe ◊, -n	cloakroom; wardrobe
die Hauptrolle, -n	main role *or* part
die Komödie, -n ▭	comedy
die Oper, -n	opera; opera house
die Reklame, -n	advertisement
die Rolle, -n	role, part
die Saison, -s ▭	season
die Schauspielerin	actress
die Schlange ◊, -n ▭	queue
die Show, -s	show
die Szene, -n	scene
die Theatergruppe, -n	dramatic society
die Tragödie, -n	tragedy

IMPORTANT WORDS (nt)

das Ballett	ballet
das Drama, Dramen	drama
das Foyer	foyer
das Kostüm ◊, -e	costume
das Kriminalstück, -e	thriller
das Make-up	make-up
das Opernglas	(pair of) opera glasses
das Orchester	orchestra; band
das Parkett ◊, -e	stalls (*pl*)
das Schauspiel, -e	play
das Schauspielhaus, (-häuser)	theatre

USEFUL WORDS (m)

der Abgang, ‥e	exit (*of actor*)
der Auftritt, -e	entrance (*of actor*); scene (*of play*)
der Beifall	applause
der Intendant, -e	stage manager
der Orchesterraum, (-räume)	orchestra pit
der Produzent ◇, -en	(film) producer
der Regisseur	producer; director
der Souffleur, -e	prompter
der Spielfilm, -e	feature film
der Spionfilm, -e	spy film

USEFUL WORDS (f)

die Farce, -n	farce
die Galerie	the "gods", gallery
die Generalprobe, -n	dress rehearsal
die Inszenierung	production
die Kapelle ◇, -n	band
die Kritik	review
die Leinwand ◇, ‥e	screen
die Loge, -n	box
die Pause ◇, -n	interval
die Platzanweiserin	usherette, attendant
die Probe, -n	rehearsal
die Schauspielkunst	acting
die Souffleuse, -n	prompter
die Tribüne ◇, -n	platform
die Zugabe, -n	encore

USEFUL WORDS (nt)

das Lustspiel, -e	comedy
das Plakat, -e	poster, notice
das Rampenlicht	footlights (*pl*)
das Scheinwerferlicht, -er	spotlight
das Trauerspiel, -e	tragedy

ESSENTIAL WORDS (m)	
der Abend, -e	evening
der Augenblick, -e	moment, instant
der Beginn	beginning
der Mittag	mid-day, noon
der Moment, -e	moment
der Monat, -e	month
der Morgen	morning
der Nachmittag	afternoon
der Tag, -e	day
der Vormittag	morning
der Wecker	alarm clock

ESSENTIAL WORDS (f)	
die Armbanduhr, -en	(wrist) watch
die Jahreszeit, -en	season
die Minute, -n	minute
die Mitte	middle
die Mitternacht	midnight
die Nacht, ¨e	night; night-time
die Sekunde, -n	second
die halbe Stunde	half-hour, half-an-hour
die Stunde ⟡, -n	hour
die Tageszeit	daytime
die Uhr ⟡, -en	clock; time
die Viertelstunde	quarter of an hour
die Weile, -n	while, short time
die Woche, -n	week
die Zeit, -en	time

ESSENTIAL WORDS (nt)	
das Datum, Daten	date
das Ende, -n	end
das Jahr, -e	year
das Jahrhundert, -e	century
das Mal, -e	time, occasion
das Wochenende, -n	weekend

um 7 Uhr aufstehen to get up at 7 o'clock
um 11 Uhr zu Bett gehen to go to bed at 11 o'clock
wieviel Uhr ist es?, wie spät ist es? what time is it?
den wievielten haben wir heute? what is today's date?
früh early; **spät** late; **bald** soon; **später** later
fast almost; **pünktlich** punctual
es ist gerade or **punkt 2 Uhr** it is exactly 2 o'clock
halb 3 half past 2; **halb 9** half past 8
gegen 8 Uhr round about 8 o'clock
es ist Viertel nach 5/Viertel vor 5 it is a quarter past 5/a
    quarter to 5

vorgestern	the day before yesterday
gestern	yesterday
am vorigen or	the day before, the
vorgehenden Tag	previous day
heute	today
heute abend	tonight
morgen	tomorrow
am nächsten or	
folgenden Tag	the next or following day
übermorgen	the day after tomorrow
am übernächsten Tag	two days later
vierzehn Tage	a fortnight

morgens in the morning	
nachmittags in the afternoon	
abends in the evening	
nachts at night, by night	
tagsüber, am Tage during the day	
stündlich hourly	
täglich daily	
wöchentlich weekly	
monatlich monthly	
jährlich annually	
heutzutage nowadays	

IMPORTANT WORDS (f)

die Essenszeit, -en	mealtime
die Gelegenheit, -en	opportunity, occasion
die Kuckucksuhr, -en	cuckoo clock
die Uhrzeit, -en	time of day

einen Augenblick! just a minute!
in diesem/dem Augenblick at this/that moment
im selben Augenblick at that very moment
ich habe keine Zeit (dazu) I have no time (for it)
(sich) die Zeit vertreiben to pass the time
es ist Zeit zum Essen it is time for lunch (dinner *etc*)
anderthalb Stunden warten to wait an hour and a half
damals at that time
nie, niemals never; **jemals** ever
diesmal this time; **ein anderes Mal** another time
nächstes Mal next time
das erste/letzte Mal the first/last time
zum ersten/letzten Mal for the first/last time
am Wochenende at the weekend
über das Wochenende for the weekend
ich habe es eilig I'm in a hurry
ich habe keine Eile I'm in no hurry
es hat keine Eile there's no hurry

USEFUL WORDS (m)	
der Einbruch der Nacht	nightfall
der Kalender	calendar
der Tagesanbruch	daybreak
der (Uhr)zeiger	hand (*of clock etc*)
der Zeitabschnitt, -e	time, period

USEFUL WORDS (f)	
die Epoche, -n	epoch, period
die Gegenwart	present (*time, tense*)
die Mittagszeit, -en	lunch time
die Pause ◇, -n	interval; pause, break
die Standuhr, -en	grandfather clock
die Stoppuhr, -en	stopwatch
die Vergangenheit	past (*time, tense*)
die Verspätung	delay (*of vehicle*)
die Zukunft	future (*time, tense*)

USEFUL WORDS (nt)	
das Futur(um)	future tense
das Jahrzehnt, -e	decade
das Mittelalter	the Middle Ages
das Präsens	present tense
das Schaltjahr, -e	leap year
das Zeitalter	age, time
das Zifferblatt, ̈-er	(clock) face, dial

vor einer Woche/einem Monat/2 Jahren a week/a month/2 years ago

gestern/heute vor einer Woche a week ago yesterday/today

gestern/heute vor 2 Jahren 2 years ago yesterday/today

in einer Woche/einem Monat/2 Jahren in a week('s time)/ a month('s time)/2 years(' time)

morgen/heute in einer Woche a week tomorrow/today

ESSENTIAL + IMPORTANT WORDS (m)	
der Bastler	handyman
der Bohrer	drill
der Dosenöffner	tin-opener
der Hammer, ⸚	hammer
der Holzhammer	mallet
der Klebstoff, -e	glue
der Korkenzieher	corkscrew
der Schlüssel	key

ESSENTIAL + IMPORTANT WORDS (f)	
die Batterie, -n	battery
die Baustelle, -n ▢	building site
die Gabel, -n	fork
die Maschine ♢, -n ▢	machine; engine
die Werkstatt, ⸚en	workshop

ESSENTIAL + IMPORTANT WORDS (nt)	
das Ding, -e	thing, object
das Do-it-yourself	do-it-yourself, D.I.Y.
das *or* der Gummi	rubber; gum
das Gummiband, ⸚er	rubber band; elastic
das Kabel	wire; cable
das Schloß ♢, ⸚sser	lock

USEFUL WORDS (nt)	
das Brett ♢, -er	plank, board; shelf
das Gerüst, -e	scaffolding
das Seil, -e	rope, cable
das Tau ♢, -e	rope
das Werkzeug, -e	tool

basteln: er kann gut basteln he is good with his hands
wozu benutzt man ...? what do you use ... for?
reparieren to repair; **etw reparieren lassen** to have sth
  repaired
nageln to nail; **sägen** to saw

USEFUL WORDS (m)	
der Bolzen	bolt
der Büchsenöffner	tin-opener
der Draht, ⁻e	wire
der Flaschenöffner	bottle-opener
der Hobel	plane
der Kleb(e)streifen	adhesive tape
der Meißel	chisel
der Nagel, ⁻	nail
der Pickel ◇	pick, pickaxe
der Pinsel	paintbrush
der Preßluftbohrer	pneumatic drill
der Schraubenschlüssel	spanner
der Schraubenzieher	screwdriver
der Schraubstock, ⁻e	vice
der Stacheldraht	barbed wire
der Stift, -e	peg
der Tesafilm ®	Sellotape ®
der Werkzeugkasten	toolbox

USEFUL WORDS (f)	
die (Draht)zange, -n	(pair of) pliers
die Feder ◇, -n	spring, coil
die Feile, -n	file
die Heftzwecke, -n	drawing pin, thumbtack
die Kelle, -n	trowel
die Leiter ◇, -n	ladder
die Libelle ◇, -n	spirit level
die Nadel, -n	needle; pin
die Planke, -n	plank
die Reißzwecke, -n	drawing pin, thumbtack
die Säge, -n	saw
die Schaufel	shovel; scoop
die Schere, -n	(pair of) scissors
die Schnur ◇, ⁻e	string, cord; wire, flex
die Schraube, -n	screw
die Wasserwaage, -n	spirit level

ESSENTIAL WORDS (m)

der Bahnhof, ¨e	railway station
der Bürgersteig, -e 🕮	pavement
der Busbahnhof, ¨e	bus or coach station
der Dom, -e	cathedral
der Laden ♢, ¨	shop
der Markt, ¨e	market
der Markttag, -e	market day
der Park, -s	(public) park
der Parkplatz, ¨e	parking place; car park
der Polizist, -en	policeman
der Turm, ¨e	tower
der Weg ♢, -e	way

ESSENTIAL WORDS (f)

die Brücke ♢, -n	bridge
die Burg, -en	castle
die Bushaltestelle, -n	bus stop
die Ecke, -n	corner, turning
die Einbahnstraße, -n 🕮	one-way street
die Fabrik, -en	factory, works
die Fahrt ♢, -en	journey
die Haltestelle, -n	(bus or tram) stop
die Hauptstraße, -n	main road; main street
die Kirche, -n	church
die Klinik, -en	hospital, clinic
die Polizei	police
die (Polizei)wache, -n	police station
die Post ♢, -en	post office
die Reise ♢, -n or	tour
die Rundfahrt, -en	tour
die Stadt, ¨e	town; city
die Straße, -n	street, road
die Straßenecke, -n	street corner
die Tankstelle, -n	service station, garage
die U-Bahn	underground (railway)

ESSENTIAL WORDS (nt)

das Büro, -s	office
das Geschäft ⟡, -e	shop
das Heft, -e	book (*of tickets*)
das Hotel, -s	hotel
das Kaufhaus, (-häuser)	department store
das Kino, -s	cinema
das Krankenhaus, ¨er	hospital
das Museum, Museen	museum
das Parken	parking
das Parkhaus, (-häuser)	(covered) car park
das Postamt, ¨er	post office
das Rathaus, (-häuser)	town hall
das Restaurant, -s	restaurant
das Schloß ⟡, ¨sser	castle
das Stadtzentrum	city centre, town centre
das Straßenschild, -er	roadsign
das Taxi, -s	taxi
das Theater	theatre
das Verkehrsamt, ¨er	tourist information centre

in die Stadt gehen *or* **fahren** to go into town
in der Stadtmitte in the centre of town
eine Stadtrundfahrt machen to go on a tour of the city
die Straße hinübergehen to cross the road
die Sehenswürdigkeiten besichtigen to have a look at the sights

---

IMPORTANT WORDS (m)

der Betrieb ◇ ▭	bustle
der Bezirk, -e ▭	district
der Biergarten, ⁼	beer garden
der Bürgermeister	mayor
der Einwohner	inhabitant
der Friedhof, ⁼e ▭	cemetery, graveyard
der Fußgänger ▭	pedestrian
der Platz ◇, ⁼e	square
der Verkehr	traffic

IMPORTANT WORDS (f)

die Aussicht, -en ▭	view
die Bürgermeisterin	mayoress
die Feuerwehrwache, -n	fire station
die Menge, -n	crowd
die Schlange ◇, -n ▭	queue
die Sehenswürdigkeiten (pl)	sights, places of interest
die Umgebung	the surroundings (pl)
die Verkehrsstauung, -en ▭	traffic jam

IMPORTANT WORDS (nt)

das Denkmal, ⁼er ▭	monument
das Fahrzeug, -e ▭	vehicle
das Gebäude ▭	building
das Tor ◇, -e	gate(way), arch

USEFUL WORDS (m)	
der **Abwasserkanal**, ⁓e	sewer
der **Bürger**	citizen
der **Fußgängerüberweg**, -e	pedestrian crossing
der **Kinderwagen**	pram
der **Landkreis**, -e	(like British) county
der **Ort**, -e	place, spot
der **Passant**, -en	passer-by
der **Pfad**, -e	path
der **Pflasterstein**, -e	paving stone
der **Rad(fahr)weg**, -e	cycle path or track
der **Staatsbürger** or	citizen
der **Stadtbewohner** or	
der **Städter**	town dweller
der **Stadtrand**	the outskirts (pl)
der **Straßenübergang**	pedestrian crossing
der **Taxistand**, ⁓e	taxi rank
der **Umzug** ◊, ⁓e	parade
der **Wegweiser**	roadsign
der **Wohnblock**, -s	block of flats
der **Wolkenkratzer**	skyscraper

in der Stadt/am Stadtrand wohnen to live in the town/in the suburbs
auf dem Platz in or on the square
an der Ecke at or on the corner
zum Markt gehen, auf den Markt gehen to go to the market
Weihnachtsmarkt Christmas fair
zu Fuß gehen to walk
mit dem Bus/mit dem Zug fahren to go by bus/by train
ein Taxi anrufen to call a taxi
ins Theater/ins Kino gehen to go to the theatre/the cinema
modern modern; **alt** old
sauber clean; **schmutzig** dirty
typisch typical
ziemlich quite; **sehr** very

USEFUL WORDS (f)	
die Bevölkerung, -en	population
die Gasse, -n	lane, back street
die Großstadt, ⸚e	city
die Kreuzung, -en	crossroads
die Kunstgalerie, -n	art gallery
die Leuchtreklame, -n	neon sign
die Meinungsumfrage, -n	opinion poll
die Prozession, -en	procession
die Sackgasse, -n	dead end
die Siedlung, -en	housing estate
die Sozialwohnung, -en	council flat *or* house
die Spitze ⬦, -n	spire
die Stadtmitte, -n	town centre; city centre
die Statue, -n	statue
die Straßenlaterne, -n	street lamp
die Tour, -en	tour
die Umgehungsstraße, -n	by-pass
die Vorstadt	suburbs (*pl*)

USEFUL WORDS (nt)

---

das Gedränge   crowd
das Kopfsteinpflaster *(sg)*   cobblestones
das Plakat, -e   poster, notice
das (Stadt)viertel   district
das Werk, -e   factory, works
das Wohngebiet   built-up area

"Betreten der Baustelle verboten" "building site: keep out"
"Anlieger frei" "residents only"
"Vorsicht: bissiger Hund!" "beware of the dog"
"Fußgängerzone" "pedestrian precinct"
"bitte freihalten" "please keep clear"
"Parken verboten" "no parking"
"Vorfahrt achten!" "give way"

ESSENTIAL WORDS (m)

der Ausgang, ¨e	exit
der Ausstieg, -e 🕮	exit (*from train*)
der Bahnhof, ¨e	station
der Bahnsteig, -e	platform
der D-Zug, ¨e (*Durchgangszug*) 🕮	through train
der Eilzug, ¨e 🕮	limited-stop train
der Eingang, ¨e	entrance
der Entwerter 🕮	ticket punching machine
der Fahrgast, ¨e 🕮	passenger
der Fahrkartenschalter	ticket *or* booking office
der Fahrplan, ¨e	timetable
der Hauptbahnhof, ¨e	main *or* central station
der Imbiß, -sse	snack
der Inter-City-Zug, ¨e 🕮	inter-city train
der Koffer	case, suitcase
der Kofferkuli, -s	luggage trolley
der Nahverkehrszug, ¨e 🕮	local train
der Passagier, -e	passenger
Reisende(r), -n	traveller
der (Reise)paß ⇨**, -pässe**	passport
der Rucksack, ¨e	rucksack, backpack
der Schnellimbiß, -sse	snack bar
der Schnellzug, ¨e	fast train, express train
der Speisewagen	dining car
der U-Bahnhof, ¨e	underground station
der Wagen ⇨	carriage, coach
der Zug ⇨**, ¨e**	train
der Zuschlag, ¨e	extra charge

ESSENTIAL WORDS (nt)

das Fundbüro, -s	lost property office
das Gepäck	luggage
das Gleis, -e	platform; track, rails
das Rad ⇨**, ¨er**	bike
das Schließfach, ¨er	left luggage locker
das Taxi, -s	taxi

ESSENTIAL WORDS (f)

die Abfahrt, -en 📖	departure
die Ankunft, ⸚e 📖	arrival
die Auskunft ◇, -̈e	information; information desk or office
die Bahn, -en	railway
die Bahnlinie, -n	railway line
die Brücke ◇, -n	bridge
Deutsche Bundesbahn (DB) 📖	German Railways
die Einfahrt, -en	entrance
die (einfache) Fahrkarte, -n	(single) ticket
die Fahrt ◇, -en	journey
die Haltestelle, -n	stop, station
die Klasse, -n	class
die Linie, -n	line
die Reise ◇, -n	journey
die Richtung, -en	direction
die Rückfahrkarte, -n	return ticket
die S-Bahn, -en 📖	high-speed railway; suburban railway
die Station ◇, -en	station
die Tasche ◇, -n	bag
die U-Bahn (*Untergrundbahn*)	underground (railway)
die U-Bahnstation, -en	underground station
die Uhr ◇, -en	clock; time

auf dem Bahnhof at the station
sich erkundigen to make inquiries
einen Platz reservieren to book a seat
nach Bonn einfach a single to Bonn
nach Bonn und zurück a return to Bonn
zweimal nach Bonn und zurück two returns to Bonn
für diese Züge muß man Zuschlag bezahlen there is an extra charge for these trains
"bitte einsteigen!" "all aboard"
"alles aussteigen!" "all change"
muß ich umsteigen? do I have to change trains?

IMPORTANT WORDS (m)

der Anschluß, ⸚sse	connection
der Aufkleber	sticker, label
der Dienst, -e	service
der Dienstwagen	guard's van
der Eisenbahner	railwayman
der Fahrausweis, -e 🔲	ticket
der Fahrschein, -e 🔲	ticket
der Gepäckwagen	luggage van
der Liegewagen	couchette
der Lokomotivführer	train driver
der Platz ✧, ⸚e	seat
der Schaffner	guard; ticket collector
der Schlafwagen	sleeping car, sleeper
Zollbeamte(r), -n	customs officer

IMPORTANT WORDS (f)

die Bahnhofsgaststätte, -n	station buffet
die Bremse, -n	brake
die Eisenbahn, -en	railway
die Gepäckaufbewahrung 🔲	left luggage office
die Grenze, -n	border, frontier
die Mehrfahrtenkarte, -n 🔲	season ticket
die Notbremse, -n 🔲	alarm, communication cord
die Verbindung, -en	connection
die Verspätung, -en	delay
die Zollkontrolle	customs control *or* check

IMPORTANT WORDS (nt)

das Abteil, -e	compartment
das Fahrgeld, -er	fare
das Gepäcknetz, -e	luggage rack
das Nichtraucherabteil, -e	non-smoking compartment
das Raucherabteil, -e	smoking compartment
das (Reise)ziel ✧, -e	destination

USEFUL WORDS (*m*)

der Anhänger ➪	label, tag
der Bahnhofsvorsteher	stationmaster
der Bahnübergang, ¨e	level crossing
der Bestimmungsort, -e	destination (*of goods*)
der Fahrpreis, -e	fare
der Gepäckträger ➪	porter
der Güterzug, ¨e	goods train
der Heizer	fireman, stoker
der Personenzug, ¨e	slow train; passenger train
der Pfiff, -e	whistle
der Schrankkoffer	trunk
der Taxistand, ¨e	taxi rank
der Vorortzug, ¨e	commuter train
der Wartesaal, (-säle)	waiting room

USEFUL WORDS (*f*)

die (Eisenbahn)schienen (*pl*)	rails
die Entgleisung, -en	derailment
die Lokomotive, -n	locomotive, engine
die Monatskarte, -n	monthly season ticket
die Nummer, -n	number
die Rolltreppe, -n	escalator
die Schranke, -n	level crossing gate
die Sperre, -n	barrier
die Strecke ➪, -n	(section of) railway line *or* track
die Wochenkarte, -n	weekly ticket

mit der Bahn by rail
den Zug erreichen/verpassen to catch/miss one's train
ist dieser Platz frei? is this seat free?
hier ist besetzt this seat is taken
"nicht hinauslehnen" "do not lean out of the window"
verspätet delayed

USEFUL WORDS (f)	
die Beere, -n	berry
die Birke, -n	birch
die Blutbuche, -n	copper beech
die Buche, -n	beech tree
die Eibe, -n	yew
die Eiche, -n	oak
die Esche, -n	ash
die Fichte, -n	spruce, pine
die Föhre, -n	Scots pine
die Kastanie, -n	chestnut; chestnut tree
die Kiefer ⟡, -n	pine
die Knospe, -n	bud
die Linde, -n	lime tree
die Mistel	mistletoe
die Pappel, -n	poplar
die Pinie, -n	pine
die Platane, -n	plane tree
die Rinde, -n	bark
die Roßkastanie, -n	horse chestnut
die Stechpalme, -n	holly
die Tanne, -n	fir tree
die Trauerweide, -n	weeping willow
die Ulme, -n	elm
die Weide ⟡, -n	willow
die Wurzel, -n	root

IMPORTANT + USEFUL WORDS (nt)	
das Blatt ⟡, ̈-er	leaf
das Geäst (*sg*)	branches
das Gebüsch (*sg*)	bushes; undergrowth
das Holz	wood (*material*)

auf einen Baum klettern to climb a tree
im Herbst werden die Blätter gelb the leaves turn yellow in autumn
im Schatten eines Baums in the shade of a tree

ESSENTIAL + IMPORTANT WORDS (m)	
der Baum, Bäume	tree
der Christbaum, (-bäume)	Christmas tree
der Forst, -e 🗀	forest
der Obstbaum, (-bäume)	fruit tree
der Obstgarten, ¨	orchard
der Schatten	shade, shadow
der Wald, ¨er	wood(s), forest
der Weihnachtsbaum, (-bäume)	Christmas tree

USEFUL WORDS (m)	
der Ahorn, -e	maple
der Ast, ¨e	branch
der Buchsbaum, (-bäume)	box tree
der Busch, ¨e	bush, shrub
der Eich(en)baum, (-bäume)	oak tree
der Kastanienbaum, (-bäume)	chestnut tree
der Kiefernzapfen	pine cone
der Lindenbaum, (-bäume)	lime tree
der Mistelzweig, -e	(sprig of) mistletoe
der Rotdorn, -e	hawthorn
der Stamm, ¨e	trunk
der Strauch, Sträucher	bush, shrub
der Tannenbaum, (-bäume)	fir tree
der Tannenzapfen	fir cone
der Weidenbaum, (-bäume)	willow
der Weinberg, -e	vineyard
der Wipfel	tree-top
der Zweig, -e	branch

ESSENTIAL WORDS (m)	
der **Champignon**, -s	(button) mushroom
der **Kohl**, -e	cabbage
der **Kopfsalat**, -e	lettuce
der **Salat** ⟡, -e	lettuce; salad

IMPORTANT WORDS (m)	
der **Blumenkohl**, -e	cauliflower
der **Knoblauch** ▭	garlic
der **Pilz**, -e	mushroom
der **Rosenkohl**	Brussels sprouts (*pl*)
der **Vegetarier**	vegetarian

USEFUL WORDS (m)	
der **Gartenkürbis**, -se	marrow
der **Kürbis**, -se	pumpkin
der **Lauch**, -e	leek
der **Mais** ⟡	sweetcorn
der **Maiskolben**	corn on the cob
der **(rote/grüne) Paprika**, (-n) -s	(red/green) pepper
der **Porree**, -s	leek
der **Rettich**, -e	(*large*) radish
der *or* die **Sellerie**	celeriac; celery
der **Spargel**	asparagus
der **Spinat**	spinach
der **Stangensellerie**	celery

Gemüse anbauen to grow vegetables
organisch organic
Salzkartoffeln (*pl*) boiled potatoes
Pellkartoffeln, Schalkartoffeln potatoes boiled in their jackets
Knoblauchwurst (*f*) garlic sausage
geraspelte Möhre grated carrot
rot wie eine Tomate as red as a beetroot
vegetarisch vegetarian

ESSENTIAL WORDS (f)

die Bohne, -n	bean
die grüne Bohne	French bean
die Erbse, -n	pea
die Kartoffel, -n	potato
die Tomate, -n	tomato
die Zwiebel, -n	onion

IMPORTANT WORDS (f)

die Aubergine, -n	aubergine
die Avocado(birne), -s/-n	avocado (pear)
die Brokkoli (pl)	broccoli
die Gurke, -n	cucumber
die Karotte, -n	carrot
die Vegetarierin	vegetarian

USEFUL WORDS (f)

die Artischocke, -n	artichoke
die Brunnenkresse	watercress
die Eierfrucht, ¨e	aubergine, eggplant
die Endivie, -n	endive
die Erdartischocke, -n	Jerusalem artichoke
die Essiggurke, -n	gherkin
die Kresse	cress
die Möhre; die Mohrrübe, -n	carrot
die Paprikaschote, -n	pepper, capsicum
die Pastinake, -n	parsnip
die Petersilie	parsley
die Rübe, -n	turnip
die rote Rübe, -n -n	beetroot
die Zucchini	courgette

ESSENTIAL + USEFUL WORDS (nt)

das Gemüse	vegetable(s)
das Kraut, Kräuter	herb; cabbage
das Radieschen	radish
das Sauerkraut	pickled cabbage

ESSENTIAL WORDS (m)	
der Bus, -se	bus
der Dampfer	steamer
der Krankenwagen	ambulance
der Lastkraftwagen (LKW) 🕮	lorry, truck; heavy goods vehicle
der Personenkraftwagen (PKW) 🕮	private car
der Polizeiwagen	police car
der Straßenbahnwagen	tramcar
der Tanker	tanker
der Wagen ⇨	car; cart; carriage
der Wohnwagen	caravan
der Zug ⇨, ̈-e	train

ESSENTIAL WORDS (f)	
die Fähre, -n 🕮	ferry
die Straßenbahn, -en	tram
die U-Bahn	underground

ESSENTIAL WORDS (nt)	
das Auto, -s	car
das Boot, -e	boat
das Fährboot, -e	ferry-boat
das Fahrrad, ̈-er	bicycle
das Flugzeug, -e	plane, aeroplane
das Mofa, -s	moped (small)
das Motorboot, -e	motorboat
das Motorrad, ̈-er	motorbike, motorcycle
das Rad ⇨, ̈-er	bike
das Ruderboot, -e	rowing boat
das Schiff, -e	ship, vessel
das Taxi, -s	taxi

reisen to travel
fahren to go
eine Reise machen to go on a journey
gute Reise! have a good trip!
mit der Bahn *or* **dem Zug fahren** to go by rail *or* by train
mit dem Auto fahren to drive, go by car
nach Frankfurt fliegen to fly to Frankfurt
zu Fuß gehen to walk, go on foot
trampen, per Anhalter fahren to hitch-hike
mit einer Höchstgeschwindigkeit von 25 Kilometern pro Stunde fahren to drive at a maximum speed of 25 kilometres per hour
seine Fahrkarte entwerten to cancel one's ticket (*in machine*)
gebrauchte Autos second-hand cars
mieten to hire
ein Mietauto (*nt*) a hired car
öffentliche Verkehrsmittel (*pl*) public transport

IMPORTANT WORDS (m)

der **Bulldozer**	bulldozer
der **Fahrpreis**, -e	fare
der **Feuerwehrwagen**	fire engine
der **Flugzeugträger**	aircraft carrier
der **Hubschrauber**	helicopter
der **Jeep**, -s	jeep
der **Kindersportwagen**	baby buggy, push-chair
der **Lieferwagen**	van; delivery van
der **Möbelwagen**	removal van, furniture van
der **(Motor)roller**	(motor) scooter
der **(Reise)bus**, -se	coach
der **Rücksitz**, -e	back seat
der **Transporter**	van; transporter
der **Vordersitz**, -e	front seat

IMPORTANT WORDS (f)

die **Autofähre**, -n 📖	car ferry
die **fliegende Untertasse**, -n -n	flying saucer
die **Gefahr**, -en 📖	danger, risk
die **Lokomotive**, -n	locomotive, engine

IMPORTANT WORDS (nt)

das **Fahrgeld**, -er	fare
das **Fahrzeug**, -e 📖	vehicle
das **Feuerwehrauto**, -s	fire engine
das **Kanu**, -s	canoe
das **Moped**	moped
das **Raumschiff**, -e	spaceship
das **Rettungsboot**, -e	lifeboat
das **Schnellboot**, -e	speedboat
das **Segelboot**, -e	sailing boat
das **UFO**	UFO (*unidentified flying object*)

USEFUL WORDS (m)	
der Anhänger ▷	trailer
der Karren	cart
der Kinderwagen	pram
der Kombiwagen	estate car, station wagon
der Lastkahn, ⁔e	barge
der (Luft)ballon, -s or -e	balloon
der Omnibus, -se	bus
der Panzer ▷	tank
der Sattelschlepper	articulated lorry
der Schleppdampfer; der	
Schlepper	tug, tugboat
der Sessellift, -e or -s	chairlift
der Streifenwagen	(police) patrol car
der Vergnügungsdampfer	pleasure steamer

USEFUL WORDS (f)	
die Dampfwalze, -n	steamroller
die Drahtseilbahn, -en	cable railway, funicular
die Düse, -n	jet (plane)
die Jacht, -en	yacht
die Planierraupe, -n	bulldozer
die Rakete, -n	rocket
die Schwebebahn, -en	cable or overhead railway

USEFUL WORDS (nt)	
das Düsenflugzeug, -e	jet plane
das Luftkissenfahrzeug, -e	hovercraft
das Paddelboot, -e	canoe
das Schlauchboot, -e	inflatable dinghy
das Segelflugzeug, -e	glider
das Tankschiff, -e	tanker
das Transportmittel	means of transport (goods)
das U-Boot, -e	
(Unterseeboot)	submarine
das Verkehrsmittel	means of transport (passengers)

The WEATHER

ESSENTIAL WORDS (m)

der Abend, -e	evening
der Berg ⌂, -e	mountain
der Blitz, -e	(flash of) lightning
der Donner	thunder
der Frost, ¨e	frost
der Frühling	spring
der Grad, -e	degree
der Herbst	autumn
der Himmel	sky; heaven
der Monat, -e	month
der Morgen	morning
der Nachmittag	afternoon
der Nebel	fog, mist
der Nord(en)	north
der Ort, -e *or* ¨er	place
der Osten	east
der Regen	rain
der Schnee	snow
der Schneesturm, ¨e	snowstorm
der Sommer	summer
der Sonnenschein	sunshine
der Sturm, ¨e	storm, gale; tempest
der Süden	south
der Westen	west
der Wind, -e	wind
der Winter	winter

blitzen to flash **(es blitzt)**
donnern to thunder **(es donnert)**
frieren to freeze **(es friert)**
gießen to pour **(es gießt)**
nieseln to drizzle **(es nieselt)**
regnen to rain **(es regnet)**
scheinen to shine **(die Sonne scheint)**
schneien to snow **(es schneit)**
es fängt an, zu schneien it's beginning to snow

ESSENTIAL WORDS (f)

die Insel, -n	island
die Jahreszeit, -en	season
die Luft	air
die Nacht, ˜e	night
die Natur	nature
die Sonne	sun
die Temperatur, -en	temperature
die Welt	world
die Wolke, -n	cloud

ESSENTIAL WORDS (nt)

das Eis ◇	ice
das Gewitter	thunderstorm
das Glatteis ▭	black ice
das Jahr, -e	year
das Land ◇, ˜er	country
das Licht, -er	light
das Wetter	weather

wie ist das Wetter heute? what's the weather like today?
wie ist das Wetter bei euch? what's the weather like with you?
wie ist die Wettervorhersage? what's the weather forecast?
heiß hot; **kalt** cold
warm warm; **kühl** cool
herrlich marvellous; **schön** lovely; **schrecklich** terrible
sonnig sunny; **windig** windy
mild mild; **rauh** harsh
schwül sultry, close; **trüb** dull
bedeckt overcast; **bewölkt** cloudy
stürmisch stormy; **neblig** misty
trocken dry; **naß** wet; **feucht** damp
heiter bright; **regnerisch** rainy

IMPORTANT WORDS (m)

der Donnerschlag, ⸚e	thunderclap
der Hagel	hail
der Mond	moon
der Mondschein	moonlight
der Niederschlag 🕮	rainfall, precipitation
der Planet, -en	planet
der Regenschauer	shower of rain
der (Regen)schirm, -e	umbrella
der Regentropfen	raindrop
der Schatten	shadow; shade
der Schauer	shower
der Schneefall, ⸚e	snowfall
der Schneeregen	sleet
der Smog	smog
der Sonnenschirm, -e	parasol, sunshade
der Stern, -e	star
der Wetterbericht, -e 🕮	weather report

IMPORTANT WORDS (f)

die Front, -en 🕮	front
die Hitze	heat
die Kälte	cold
die Verbesserung, -en	improvement
die Wetterlage 🕮	weather situation
die Wettervorhersage, -n 🕮	weather forecast

IMPORTANT WORDS (nt)

das Halbdunkel	semi-darkness
das Klima, -s *or* -te	climate
das Mondlicht	moonlight
das Sauwetter	awful weather

herrschen to prevail; **zeitweise** for a time
vereinzelt bewölkt with (occasional) cloudy patches
plus plus; **minus** minus
so ein Sauwetter! what awful weather!

USEFUL WORDS (m)

der Blitzableiter	lightning conductor
der Dunst	haze
der Eiszapfen	icicle
der Gefrierpunkt	freezing point
der Orkan, ⁻e	hurricane
der Platzregen	downpour
der Regenbogen	rainbow
der Schaden, ⁻	damage
der Sonnenaufgang, ⁻e	sunrise
der Sonnenstrahl, -en	ray of sunshine
der Sonnenuntergang, ⁻e	sunset
der Tagesanbruch	dawn, break of day
der Tau ◊	dew
der Windstoß, ⁻e	gust of wind

USEFUL WORDS (f)

die Atmosphäre	atmosphere
die Aufheiterungen (pl)	bright periods
die Bö, -en	squall, gust of wind
die Brise, -n	breeze
die Dürre, -n	(period of) drought
die Flut ◊, -en	flood
die Hitzewelle, -n	heat wave
die Kältewelle, -n	cold spell
die (Morgen)dämmerung	dawn
die Pfütze, -n	puddle
die Schneeflocke, -n	snowflake
die Schneewehe, -n	snowdrift
die Überschwemmung, -en	flood, deluge

USEFUL WORDS (nt)

das Barometer	barometer
das (Schnee)gestöber	flurry of snow
das Tauwetter	thaw
das Unwetter	thunderstorm
das Zwielicht	twilight

ESSENTIAL WORDS (m)

der Empfang 📖	reception
der Herbergsvater	warden
der Junge, -n	boy
der Rucksack, ‑e	backpack, rucksack
der Schlafsack, ‑e	sleeping bag
der Spaziergang, ‑e	walk
der Speisesaal	dining room
der Stadtplan, ‑e	street map
der Urlaub, -e	holiday(s)

ESSENTIAL WORDS (f)

die Anmeldung ⇔ 📖	registration
die Dusche, -n	shower
die Herbergsmutter	(female) warden
die Jugendherberge, -n	youth hostel
die Küche ⇔, -n	kitchen
die Landkarte, -n	map
die Mahlzeit, -en	meal
die Toilette, -n	toilet
die Übernachtung, -en	overnight stay

ESSENTIAL WORDS (nt)

das Abendessen	dinner, evening meal
das Badezimmer	bathroom
das Bett, -en	bed
das Büro, -s	office
das Essen ⇔	food; meal
das Frühstück	breakfast
das Mädchen	girl

IMPORTANT WORDS (m)
---

der Aufenthalt	stay
der Feuerlöscher 📖	fire extinguisher
der Mülleimer	dustbin
der Prospekt, -e	leaflet, brochure
der Schlafsaal, (-säle)	dormitory
der Zimmernachweis 📖	accommodation office

IMPORTANT WORDS (f)
---

die Bettwäsche	bed linen, bedclothes
die Mitgliedskarte, -n	membership card
die Münzwäscherei	launderette
die Nachtruhe 📖	lights-out
die Ruhe ◇	peace; rest
die Unterkunft, (-künfte)	accommodation
die Veranstaltung, -en 📖	organization
die Wäsche	washing (*things*)

IMPORTANT WORDS (nt)
---

das Schwarze Brett 📖	notice board

bleiben to stay
übernachten to spend the night
sich anmelden to register
mieten to hire
"Hausordnung für Jugendherbergen" "youth hostel rules"

The vocabulary items on pages 206 to 229 have been grouped under parts of speech rather than topics because they can apply in a wide range of circumstances. Use them just as freely as the vocabulary already given.

ADJECTIVES

abgenutzt worn out (*object*)
abscheulich hideous
ähnlich (+ *dat*) similar (to), like
aktuell topical
albern silly, foolish
allerlei all kinds of
allgemein general
alltäglich ordinary; daily
alt old
amüsant amusing
andere(r, s) other
anders different
angenehm pleasant
angrenzend neighbouring
arm poor
artig well-behaved, good
aufgeregt excited
aufgeweckt bright, lively
aufrichtig sincere
ausführlich detailed, elaborate
ausgestreckt stretched (out)
ausgezeichnet excellent
ausschließlich sole, exclusive
außerordentlich extraordinary
befriedigend satisfactory
begeistert keen, enthusiastic
belebt busy (*street*)
beleuchtet illuminated,

flood-lit
beliebt popular
bemerkenswert remarkable
benachbart neighbouring
bereit ready
berühmt famous
beschäftigt (mit) busy (with) (*of person*)
besetzt engaged; taken
besondere(r, s) special
besorgt worried, anxious
besser better
betrunken drunk
beunruhigt worried, disturbed
blöd silly, stupid
breit wide, broad
bunt colourful
dankbar grateful
dauernd perpetual, constant
delikat delicate; delicious
deutlich clear; distinct
dicht thick, dense
dick thick
doof daft, stupid
dreckig dirty, filthy
dringend urgent
dumm silly, stupid; annoying
dunkel dark
dünn thin
dynamisch dynamic

echt real, genuine
ehemalig old, former
ehrlich sincere, honest
eifrig keen, enthusiastic
eigen own
einfach simple; single
einzeln single, individual
einzig only
elegant elegant, smart
elektrisch, Elektro- electric
elend poor, wretched
End- final
endgültig final, definite
endlos endless
eng narrow; tight
entschlossen firm, determined
entsetzlich dreadful
entzückend delightful
erfahren experienced
ernst serious, solemn
ernsthaft serious, earnest
erreichbar reachable, within reach
erschöpft exhausted, worn out
erste(r, s) first
erstaunlich amazing, extraordinary
erstaunt astonished
fähig (zu or + *gen*) capable (of)
falsch false; wrong
faul rotten; lazy
feierlich solemn
fein fine
fern far-off, distant
fertig prepared, ready
fest firm, hard

fett fat; greasy
finster dark
flach flat
fortgeschritten advanced
fortwährend continual, endless
frech cheeky
frei free, vacant
frisch fresh
furchtbar frightful
fürchterlich terrible, awful
ganz whole, complete
geduldig patient
geeignet suitable
gefährlich dangerous
gefroren frozen
geheim secret
geheimnisvoll mysterious
gemischt mixed
gemütlich comfortable
genau exact, precise
gerade straight; even
geringste(r, s) slightest, least
gesamt whole, entire
geschichtlich historical
gewaltig tremendous, huge
gewalttätig violent
gewiß certain
gewöhnlich usual; ordinary; common
glatt smooth
gleich same; equal
glücklich happy; fortunate
gnädig gracious
gnädige Frau Madam
graziös graceful
grob coarse, rude
groß big, great, large; tall

großartig magnificent
günstig suitable, convenient
gut good
hart hard
häßlich ugly
Haupt- main
heftig fierce, violent
heiß hot
hell pale; bright, light
herrlich marvellous
historisch historical
hoch high
höflich polite, civil
hübsch pretty
intelligent intelligent
interessant interesting
jede(r, s) each, every
jung young
kalt cold
kein no, not any
klar clear, sharp
klatschnaß wet through,
 soaking wet
klein small, little
klug wise, clever
komisch funny
kompliziert complicated
körperlich physical
kostbar expensive; precious
kostenlos free (of charge)
köstlich delicious
kräftig strong
kühl cool
kurz short
lächelnd smiling
lächerlich ridiculous
lahm lame
Landes- national
lang long; tall (of person)

langsam slow
langweilig boring
laut loud, noisy
lebendig alive; lively
lebhaft lively (of person)
lecker delicious, tasty
leer empty
leicht easy; light (weight)
leidenschaftlich passionate
leise quiet; soft
letzte(r, s) last, latest; final
lieb dear
Lieblings- favourite
linke(r, s) left
lustig amusing; cheerful
sich lustig machen über
 (+ acc) to make fun of
luxuriös luxurious
Luxus- luxury, luxurious
mächtig powerful, mighty
mager thin
mehrere several
merkwürdig strange, odd
Militär-, militärisch military
mindeste least
mitleidig sympathetic
modern modern
möglich possible
müde tired
munter lively
mutig courageous
mysteriös mysterious
nächste(r, s) next; nearest
nah(e) near; close
natürlich natural
nett nice, kind
neu new
neugierig curious
niedrig low

nötig necessary
notwendig necessary
nützlich useful
nutzlos useless
obligatorisch compulsory, obligatory
offen open; frank, sincere
offenbar, offensichtlich obvious
öffentlich public
offiziell official
ordentlich (neat and) tidy
Orts- local
pädagogisch educational
passend suitable
persönlich personal
populär popular
prächtig magnificent
privat private; personal
privilegiert privileged
pünktlich punctual
Quadrat-, quadratisch square
rauh rough; harsh
rechte(r, s) right
reich rich
reif ripe
rein clean
reizend charming
religiös religious
reserviert reserved
richtig right, correct
riesig huge, gigantic
romantisch romantic
ruhig quiet, peaceful
rund round
sanft gentle, soft
satt full (*person*)
ich habe es satt I'm fed up (with it)

sauber clean
scharf sharp; spicy
schattig shady
scheu shy
schick smart, chic
schläfrig sleepy
schlank slender, slim
schlau cunning, sly
schlecht bad
schlimm bad
schmal narrow; slender
schmutzig dirty
schnell fast, quick, rapid
schön beautiful
schrecklich terrible; frightful
schroff steep; jagged; brusque
schüchtern shy
schwach weak
schweigsam silent
schwer heavy; serious
schwierig difficult
seltsam strange, odd, curious
sicher sure; safe
sichtbar visible
solche such
Sonder- special
sonderbar strange, odd
sorgenfrei carefree
sorgfältig careful
spannend exciting
Stadt-, städtisch municipal, urban
ständig perpetual
stark strong; heavy
steif stiff
steil steep
still quiet, still
stolz (auf + *acc*) proud (of)

streng severe, harsh; strict
süß sweet
sympathisch likeable
tapfer brave
technisch technical
tief deep
toll mad; terrific
tot dead
tragbar portable
traurig sad
treu true (*friend etc*)
trocken dry
typisch typical
übel wicked, bad
übrig left-over
unartig naughty
unbekannt unknown
uneben uneven
unerträglich unbearable
ungeheuer huge
ungezogen rude
unglaublich incredible
unglücklich unhappy;
  unfortunate
unheimlich weird
unmöglich impossible
ursprünglich original
verantwortlich responsible
verboten prohibited,
  forbidden
verlegen embarrassed
verletzt injured
vernünftig sensible,
  reasonable
verrückt mad, crazy
verschieden various;
  different
verständlich understandable
viereckig square
volkstümlich popular (*of the
  people*)
voll (+ *gen*) full (of)
vollkommen perfect,
  complete
vollständig complete
vorderste(r, s) front (*row
  etc*)
wach awake
wahr true
warm warm
weich soft
weise wise
weit wide
wert worth
wichtig important
wild fierce, wild
wohlhabend well-off
wunderbar wonderful,
  marvellous
zäh tough
zahlreich numerous
zart gentle, tender
zig umpteen
zufrieden satisfied,
  contented
zusätzlich extra

ADVERBS

Many other adverbs have the same form as the adjective.

absichtlich deliberately, on purpose
allein alone, on one's own
allerdings certainly; of course, to be sure
anders otherwise; differently
äußerst extremely, most
bald soon; almost
besonders especially, particularly
am besten best, best of all
bestimmt definitely, for sure
bloß only, merely
da there; here; then
daher from there; from that
dahin (to) there; then
damals at that time
danach after that; afterwards
dann then
darin in it, in there
deshalb therefore, for that reason
doch after all
dort there
dorthin (to) there
draußen out of doors; outside
drinnen inside; indoors
drüben over there, on the other side
durchaus thoroughly, absolutely
eben exactly; just
eher sooner; rather

eigentlich really, actually
einmal once; one day, some day
auf einmal all at once
endlich at last, finally
erst first; only (time)
erstens first(ly), in the first place
etwa about; perhaps
fast almost, nearly
früh early
ganz quite; completely
gar nicht not at all
gegenwärtig at present, at the moment
genau exactly, precisely
genug enough
gerade just, exactly
geradeaus straight ahead
gern(e) willingly; gladly
gewöhnlich usually
glücklicherweise fortunately
gut well
häufig frequently
heutzutage nowadays
hier here
hierher this way, here
hin und her to and fro
hinten at the back, behind
höchst highly, extremely
hoffentlich I hope, hopefully
immer always
immer noch still
inzwischen meanwhile, in the meantime

irgendwo(hin) (to) somewhere
je ever
jedenfalls in any case
jedesmal each time, every time
jedesmal wenn whenever
je ... desto: je mehr desto besser the more the better
jemals ever; at any time
jetzt now
kaum hardly, scarcely
keineswegs in no way; by no means
komischerweise funnily (enough), in a funny way
künftig in future
lange for a long time
langsam slowly
lauter (*with pl*) nothing but, only
leider unfortunately
lieber rather, preferably
am liebsten most (of all), best (of all)
links left; on *or* to the left
manchmal sometimes
mehr more
meinetwegen for my sake; on my account
am meisten (the) most
meistens mostly, for the most part
mitten (in) in the middle *or* midst (of)
möglichst as ... as possible
nachher afterwards
natürlich naturally
neu newly; afresh, anew
neu füllen *etc* to refill *etc*

nicht not
nichtsdestoweniger nevertheless
nie, niemals never
noch still; yet
noch einmal (once) again
normalerweise normally
nun now
nur just, only
oben above; upstairs
oft often
plötzlich suddenly
recht haben to be right
rechts right; on *or* to the right
richtig correctly; really
rundherum round about, all (a)round
schlecht badly
schließlich finally
schon already
schnell quickly
sehr very, a lot, very much
selbst even
selten seldom, rarely
so so, thus, like this
sofort at once, immediately
sogar even
sogleich at once, straight away
sonst otherwise; or else
spät late
überall(hin) everywhere
übrigens besides, by the way
umher about, around
ungefähr about, approximately
unten below; downstairs; at the bottom
unterwegs on the way

viel much, a lot
vielleicht perhaps, maybe
völlig completely
vorbei by, past
vorher before, previously, beforehand
wahrscheinlich probably
wann(?) when(?)
warum(?) why(?)
weit far
wie(?), wie! how(?), how!
wieder again

wirklich really
wo/woher/wohin/ wovon(?) where/from where/(to) where/from where(?)
ziemlich fairly, rather
zu to
zuerst first; at first
zufällig(?) by chance; by any chance(?)
zurück back
zweitens second(ly), in the second place

SOME MORE NOUNS!

---

das Abenteuer adventure
der Abhang, ⁻e slope
die Abkürzung, -en
  abbreviation; short-cut
der Abschnitt, -e section
die Absicht, -en intention
der Abstieg descent
die Abteilung, -en
  department, section
die Abwesenheit absence
die Ahnung, -en idea,
  suspicion
die Änderung, -en
  alteration, change
der Anfang, ⁻e beginning
zu Anfang at the beginning
die Angst, ⁻e fear
ich habe Angst (vor + dat)
  I am afraid or frightened
  (of)
die Anmeldung ⇨, -en
  announcement
die Anstalten (fpl)
  preparations
die Anstrengung, -en effort
die Antwort, -en answer, reply
die Anweisungen (fpl)
  orders, instructions
die Anwesenheit presence
das Anzeichen sign,
  indication
die Anzeige, -n advertisement
der Apparat, -e machine
das Ärgernis, -se annoyance
die Art, -en way, method;
  kind, sort
auf meine Art in my own way

aller Art of all kinds
der Aufenthalt, -e stay
die Aufmerksamkeit
  attention; attentiveness
die Aufsicht supervision
der Aufstieg ascent
der Ausdruck, ⁻e term,
  expression
die Auseinandersetzung,
  -en argument
der Ausgangspunkt, -e
  starting point
die Ausnahme, -n exception
die Ausstellung, -en
  exhibition
die Auswahl, en (an + dat)
  selection (of)
der Bau construction
die Beaufsichtigung
  supervision
die Bedeutung, -en
  meaning; importance
die Bedingung, -en
  condition, stipulation
das Bedürfnis, -se need
der Befehl, -e order,
  command
die Begabung, -en talent
der Begriff: im Begriff sein,
  etw zu tun to be busy doing
  sth
das Beispiel, -e example
zum Beispiel for example
die Bemerkung, -en remark
die Bemühung, -en trouble,
  effort
die Berechnung, -en

calculation

der Bescheid, -e message, information

jdm Bescheid sagen to let sb know

sein Bestes tun to do one's best

der Betrag, ⁼e sum, amount (of money)

der Blödsinn nonsense

die Botschaft, -en message, news; embassy

die Breite, -n width

der Bursche, -n fellow

die Chance, -n chance, opportunity

der Dank thanks (pl)

die Darstellung, -en portrayal, representation

das Denken thinking, thought

das Diagramm, -e diagram

die Dicke, -n thickness; fatness

der Dienst, -e service

die Dimension, -en dimension

das Ding, -e thing, object

der Duft, ⁼e smell, fragrance

die Dummheit, -en stupidity; stupid mistake

der Dummkopf, ⁼e idiot

der Dunst, ⁼e vapour

die Ecke, -n corner

die Ehre, -n honour

die Einbildung, -en imagination

der Eindruck, ⁼e impression

der Einfall, ⁼e thought, idea

die Einzelheit, -en detail

die Eleganz elegance

der Empfang, ⁼e reception

die Empfindung, -en feeling, emotion

das Ende, -n end

zu Ende gehen to end

die Entschlossenheit resolution, determination

das Ereignis, -se event

die Erfahrung, -en experience

der Erfolg, -e result; success

das Ergebnis, -se result

die Erinnerung, -en memory, remembrance

die Erklärung, -en explanation

die Erkundigung, -en inquiry

die Erlaubnis, -se permission; permit

das Erlebnis, -se experience

der Ernst earnestness, seriousness

im Ernst in earnest

das Erstaunen astonishment

die Erwiderung, -en retort

das Exil, -e exile (state)

der Feind, -e enemy

die Folge, -n order; series; result

die Form, -en form, shape

die Frage, -n question

Fremde(r), -n, die Fremde, -n stranger; foreigner

die Freude, -n joy, delight

die Freundlichkeit, -en kindness

der Frieden peace
die Frische freshness
der Führer guide; leader
die Gebühr, -en fee, charge
das Gedächtnis, -se memory
der Gedanke, -n thought, idea
die Geduld patience
die Gefahr, -en danger
der Gegenstand, -̈e object
das Gegenteil, -e opposite
im Gegenteil on the contrary
die Gegenwart present
das Geheimnis, -se mystery; secret
die Gelegenheit, -en opportunity, occasion
das Gemisch, -e mixture
das Gerät, -e device, tool
das Geräusch, -e sound, noise
der Geruch, -̈e smell
das Geschick, -e fate; skill
der Geselle, -n fellow
der Gesichtspunkt, -e point of view
die Gewandtheit skill
das Glück luck; prosperity; happiness
der Gott, -̈er god
der (liebe) Gott God
der Grund ◇, -̈e reason
die Gruppe, -n group
die Grüße (mpl) wishes
die Güte kindness
die Hauptsache, -n the main thing

die Herstellung, -en manufacture
die Hilfe help
der Hintergrund background
das Hin und Her coming(s) and going(s)
die Hoffnung, -en hope
die Höflichkeit, -en politeness
die Höhe, -n height; level
die Idee, -n idea
das Interesse, -n interest
der Kampf, -̈e fight, battle
die Kapelle ◇, -n chapel
das Kapitel chapter
die Katastrophe, -n disaster, catastrophe
die Kenntnis, -se knowledge
der Kerl, -e fellow, chap
die Kette, -n chain
der Klang, -̈e sound
die Klimaanlage air-conditioning
die Konstruktion, -en construction
die Kontrolle, -n control, supervision
die Kopie, -n copy
der Korb, -̈e basket
die Kosten cost(s); expenses
der Kreis, -e circle; district
der Krieg, -e war
das Lächeln smile
die Lage, -n situation
der Landstreicher tramp
die Länge, -n length
die Lang(e)weile boredom
der Lärm noise
der Laut, -e sound

NOUNS

das **Leben** life
das **Leid** sorrow, grief
der **Leiter** chief, leader
der **Leser**, die **Leserin** reader
das **Licht**, -er light
die **Liebe**, -n love
die **Linie**, -n line
die **Liste**, -n list
die **Literatur** literature
das **Loch**, ¨er hole
die **Lösung**, -en solution
die **Lücke**, -n opening, gap
die **Lüge**, -n lie
die **Lust: ich habe Lust, es zu tun** I feel like doing it
die **Macht**, ¨e power
das **Magazin**, -e magazine
der **Mangel**, ¨ (an + dat) lack (of), shortage (of)
die **Mark** (German) mark
die **Maschine**, -n machine; engine
das **Maximum** -a maximum
die **Meinung**, -en opinion, view
meiner Meinung nach in my opinion
das **meiste; die meisten** most
die **Meldung**, -en announcement
die **Menge**, -n crowd; quantity, lot
das **Minimum**, -a minimum
die **Mischung**, -en mixture
das **Mißgeschick**, -e misfortune
das **Mitleid** sympathy

die **Mitteilung**, -en communication
das **Mittel** means; method
das **Modell**, -e model, version
die **Möglichkeit**, -en means; possibility
sein Möglichstes tun to do one's best
die **Mühe** pains, trouble
die **Münze**, -n coin
der **Mut** courage, spirit
die **Nachrichten** (fpl) news; information
der **Nachteil**, -e disadvantage
die **Nähe: in der Nähe** close by
das **Netz**, -e network
die **Not** need, distress
die **Notiz**, -en note, item
die **Nummer**, -n number
das **Objekt**, -e object
die **Öffentlichkeit** the general public
die **Öffnung**, -en opening
die **Ordnung**, -en order
in Ordnung bringen to arrange, tidy (up)
alles ist in Ordnung everything is all right
der **Ort**, -e place
das **Pech**, -e misfortune, bad luck
der **Pfeil**, -e arrow
das **Pfund**, -e pound (sterling); pound (weight)
der **Plan**, ¨e plan; map
der **Platz** ⬦, ¨e place; seat;

room, space; square
die Plauderei, -en chat, conversation; talk
die Politik politics; policy
das Porträt, -s portrait
das Problem, -e problem
das Produkt, -e product; produce
die Publizität publicity
der Punkt, -e point; dot; full stop
die Puppe, -n doll
die Qualität, -en quality
der Radau hullaballoo
der Rand, ̈er edge; rim
der Rat, -schläge (piece of) advice
das Rätsel puzzle, riddle
der Rauch smoke
der Raum ♢, Räume space; room
die Rede, -n speech
eine Rede halten to make a speech
die Regierung, -en government; reign
die Reihe, -n series; line
ich bin an der Reihe it's my turn now
der Reiz, -e attraction, charm
die Reklame, -n advertisement
der Rest remainder, rest
die Reste (mpl) remains, remnants
das Resultat, -e result
der Revolutionär, -e revolutionary
der Rhythmus, -men rhythm

die Richtung, -en direction
die Rückseite, -n back (of page etc)
der Ruf, -e call, cry; reputation
die Ruhe rest; peace; calm; silence
die Sache, -n thing; matter
der Schein, -e (bank) note
ein 20 Mark Schein a 20-mark note
das Schicksal fate
das Schild, -er sign; label
der Schlag, ̈e blow, knock
der Schluß, ̈sse end(ing)
am Schluß at the end
der Schmutz, die Schmutzigkeit dirt, dirtiness
der Schrei, -e cry, scream
der Schritt, -e footstep; step; pace
die Schuld fault
ich bin nicht schuld daran it's not my fault
die Schwierigkeit, -en difficulty
die Sensation stir, sensation
die Serie, -n series
die Sicherheit security; safety
die Sicht sight; view
der Sieg, -e victory
der Sinn, -e mind; sense; meaning
die Situation, -en situation
die Sorge, -n care, worry
sich Sorgen machen to be worried
die Sorte, -n sort, kind

das Souvenir, -s souvenir
der Spalt crack, opening; split
die Spalte, -n column (of page)
der Spaß ◇, ⁻e fun; joke
der Spektakel hullaballoo
das Spielzeug, -e toy
die Spur, -en sign, trace
der Staat, -en state
der Standpunkt, -e point of view, standpoint
die Stärke power, strength
die Stelle ◇, -n place
die Steuer, -n tax
der Stil, -e style
die Stille stillness
die Stimmung, -en mood; atmosphere
die Strecke ◇, -n stretch; distance
das Stück ◇, -e piece, part
die Summe, -n sum
das System, -e system
das Talent talent
die Tat, -en act, action, deed
in der Tat in (actual) fact, indeed
die Tätigkeit, -en activity
der Teil, -e, das Teil, -e part, section
der Text, -e text
der Titel title
die Tiefe, -n depth
der Tor ◇, -en fool
der Traum, ⁻e dream
der Treffpunkt, -e meeting place
der Trost comfort
die Trümmer (pl) wreckage; ruins
der Typ, -en type
der Überlebende(r), -n, die Überlebende, -n survivor
die Überraschung, -en surprise
die Umgebung, -en surroundings (pl)
das Unglück misfortune; bad luck; disaster
das Unheil evil; disaster, misfortune
das Unrecht: Unrecht haben to be wrong, be mistaken
die Unterbrechung, -en interruption
die Unterhaltung, -en conversation, chat
das Unternehmen undertaking, enterprise
der Unterschied, -e difference
der Urlaub, -e holidays, leave
die Ursache reason, cause
die Verabredung, -en appointment
die Verbindung, -en connection
der Vergleich, -e comparison
das Vergnügen pleasure
der Versuch ◇, -e attempt
das Vertrauen confidence
die Vorbereitung, -en preparation
der Vorschlag, ⁻e suggestion
die Vorsicht care, caution
die Vorstellung

introduction; idea, thought

der Vorteil, -e advantage

die Wahl, -en choice, selection; election

der Wähler voter

die Wahrheit truth

der Wechselkurs, -e exchange rate

die Weile, -n while

die Weise, -n way, method, manner

auf diese Weise in this way *or* manner

die Weite width; distance

die Werbung, -en advertising

der Wert, -e value

die Wette, -n bet

die Wichtigkeit importance

die Wirklichkeit, -en fact, reality

die Wirkung, -en effect

der Witz, -e joke

der Wohlstand prosperity

das Wort, ¨er *or* **-e** word

der Wunsch, ¨e wish

die Wut rage, fury

die Zahl, -en number, figure

das Zeichen sign

die Zeile, -n line (*of text*)

die Zeitschrift, -en magazine

die Zeitung, -en newspaper

das Zentrum, Zentren centre

das Zeug stuff; gear

das Ziel, -e aim, goal; destination

die Ziffer, -n number, figure

der Zorn anger

der Zweck, -e purpose

PREPOSITIONS AND CONJUNCTIONS

---

aber but; however
als when; as; than
als ob, als wenn as if, as though
also therefore, so
anstatt (+ *gen*) instead of
außer (+ *dat*) out of; except
außerhalb (+ *gen*) outside
bei (+ *dat*) near, by; at the house of
bevor before (*time*)
bis until, till (*conj*); (+ *acc*) until; (up) to, as far as
da as, since, seeing (that)
damit so that, in order that
denn for
ehe before
entweder ... oder either ... or
gegenüber (+ *dat*) opposite; to(wards)
gerade als just as
indem as, while
innerhalb (+ *gen*) in(side), within
je ..., desto the more ... the more
nachdem after
nun (da) now (that)

ob if, whether
obwohl although
oder or
ohne daß without
seit (+ *dat*) since
sobald as soon as
so daß so that
solange as long as
sondern (*after neg*) but
nicht nur ... sondern auch not only ... but also
sowohl ... als (auch) both ... and
statt (+ *gen*) instead of
teils ... teils partly ... partly
trotz (+ *gen*) despite, in spite of
und and
während while (*conj*); (+ *gen*) during (*prep*)
weder ... noch neither ... nor
wegen (+ *gen*) because of
weil because
wenn when; if
wenn ... auch although; even if
wie as, like

VERBS

abhängen von to depend on
abholen to fetch, go and meet (*somebody*)
ablehnen to refuse
abschreiben to copy
akzeptieren to accept
anbeten to adore
anbieten to give, offer
anblicken to look (at)
ändern: seine Meinung ändern to change one's mind
anfangen to begin
angeben to state
angehören (+ *dat*) to belong to (*club etc*)
angreifen to attack; to touch
anhalten to stop; to continue
ankommen to arrive
ankündigen to announce
annehmen to accept; to assume
anschalten to switch on
antworten to answer, reply
anzeigen to announce
anziehen to attract; to put (on) (*clothes*)
sich ärgern to get angry
aufbewahren to keep, store
aufhängen to hang (up)
aufheben to raise, lift
aufhören to stop (*intransitive*)
aufkleben to stick on *or* onto
aufmachen to open
aufpassen (auf + *acc*) to watch; to be careful (of), pay attention (to)

aufstehen to get up
auftreten to appear (*on the scene*)
aufwachen to wake up (*intransitive*)
aufwärmen to warm (up)
aufwecken to awaken, wake up (*transitive*)
ausdrücken to express
ausführen to carry out, execute
ausgeben to spend (*money*)
auslöschen to put out, extinguish
ausrufen to exclaim, cry (out)
sich ausruhen to rest
ausschalten to switch off
ausschlafen to have a good sleep
aussprechen to pronounce
ausstrecken to extend, hold out
sich ausstrecken to stretch out
auswählen to select
beabsichtigen to intend
beachten to observe, obey
sich (bei jdm) bedanken to say thank you (to sb)
bedecken to cover
bedeuten to mean
bedienen to serve; to operate
sich beeilen to hurry
beenden to finish
befehlen (+ *dat*) to order
sich befinden to be
begegnen (+ *dat*) to meet

beginnen to begin
begreifen to realize
behalten to keep, retain
behaupten to maintain
beherrschen to rule (over)
sich beklagen (über + *acc*) to complain (about)
bekommen to obtain
bemerken to notice
benachrichtigen to inform
benutzen to use
beobachten to watch
berichten to report
(sich) beruhigen to calm down
sich beschäftigen mit to attend to; to be concerned with
beschmutzen to dirty
beschreiben to describe
(be)schützen (vor + *dat*) to protect (from)
besiegen to conquer
besitzen to own, possess
besprechen to discuss
bestehen (aus + *dat*) to consist (of), comprise
bestehen (auf + *dat*) to insist (upon)
bestellen to order
besuchen to attend, be present at, go to, visit
betreten to enter
beunruhigen to worry, disturb
(sich) bewegen to move
bewundern to admire
biegen to bend
bieten to offer

binden to tie
bitten to request
bitten um to ask for
bleiben to stay, remain
blicken (auf + *acc*) to glance (at), look (at)
borgen to borrow; **jdm etw borgen** to lend sb sth
brauchen to need
brechen to break
brennen to burn
bringen to bring, take
bummeln to wander; to skive
danken (+ *dat*) to thank
darstellen to represent
dauern to last
decken to cover
denken to think, believe
denken an (+ *acc*) to think of; to remember
denken über (+ *acc*) to think about; to reflect on
deuten (auf + *acc*) to point (to *or* at)
dienen to serve
diskutieren to discuss
drehen to turn; to shoot (*film*)
drucken to print
drücken to press, squeeze
durchführen to accomplish, carry out
durchqueren to cross, pass through
durchsuchen to search (all over)
dürfen to be allowed to
eilen to rush, dash
einfallen (+ *dat*) to occur (to *someone*)

einladen to invite
einrichten to establish, set up
einschalten to switch on
einschlafen to fall asleep
eintreten to come in
eintreten in (+ *acc*) to come into, enter
einwickeln to wrap (up)
empfangen to receive (*person*)
empfehlen to recommend
entdecken to discover
entführen to take away
enthalten to contain
(sich) entscheiden to decide
sich entschließen to make up one's mind
entschuldigen to excuse
sich entschuldigen (für) to apologize (for)
(sich) entwickeln to develop
sich ereignen to happen
erfahren to learn; to experience; **erfahren von** to hear about
ergreifen to seize
erhalten to receive, get
sich erheben to rise
erinnern (an + *acc*) to remind (of)
sich erinnern (an + *acc*) to remember
erkennen to recognize
erklären to state; to explain
sich erkundigen (nach *or* **über** + *acc*) to inquire about
erlauben to allow, permit, let
erleben to experience

ermutigen to encourage
erobern to capture
erregen to disturb, excite
erreichen to reach; to catch (*train etc*)
errichten to erect
erschaffen to create
erscheinen to appear
erschrecken to frighten
erschüttern to shake, rock, stagger
erstaunen to astonish
erwachen to wake up (*intransitive*)
erwähnen to mention
erwarten to expect, await, wait for
erwidern to retort
erzählen to tell, explain
erziehen to bring up, educate
fallen to fall
fallen lassen to drop
falten to fold
fangen to catch
fassen to grasp; to comprehend
fehlen to be missing; **er fehlt mir** I miss him
etw fertigmachen to bring sth about; to get sth ready
festbinden to tie, fasten
finden to find
fliehen (vor + *dat*, **aus)** to flee (from)
fließen (in + *acc*) to flow (into)
flüstern to whisper
folgen (+ *dat*) to follow
fordern to demand

VERBS

fortgehen to go away
fortfahren (vor + dat) to depart; to continue
fortsetzen to continue (*transitive*)
fragen to ask
sich fragen to wonder
sich freuen to be glad
führen to lead
füllen to fill
funkeln to sparkle
funktionieren to work (*of machine*)
sich fürchten (vor + dat) to be afraid *or* frightened (of)
geben to give
gebrauchen to use
gefallen (+ dat) to please; **das gefällt mir** I like that
gehen to go
gehorchen (+ dat) to obey
gehören (+ dat) to belong (to)
gelingen to succeed
gelten to be worth
genießen to enjoy
genügen to be sufficient
gernhaben to like
geschehen to happen
gestatten to permit, allow
glauben (+ dat) to believe
glauben an (+ acc) to believe in
glühen to glow
gründen to establish
gucken to look
haben to have
halten to keep; to stop; to hold

halten für to consider (as)
handeln: es handelt sich um it is a question of
hangen to be hanging
hängen to hang (up)
hassen to hate, loathe
hauen to cut, hew
heben to lift, raise
helfen (+ dat) to help
herantreten an (+ acc) to approach
herausziehen to pull out
hereinkommen to enter, come in
hereinlassen to admit
herstellen to produce, manufacture
herunterlassen to lower
hineingehen (in + acc) to enter, go in (to)
hinlegen to put down
sich hinsetzen to sit down
hinstellen to put down
hinübergehen to go through; to go over
hinweisen to point out
hinweisen auf (+ acc) to refer to
hinzufügen to add
hoffen (auf + acc) to hope (for)
holen to fetch
horchen to listen
hören to hear
hüten to guard, watch over
interessieren to interest
sich für etw interessieren to be interested in sth
sich irren to be mistaken

kämpfen to fight
kennen to know (*person, place*)
kennenlernen to meet, get to know
klagen to complain
klatschen to gossip
klettern to climb
klingeln to ring
klingen to sound
kochen to cook
kommen to come
können to be able (to)
kriegen to get, obtain
sich kümmern (um) to worry (about)
küssen to kiss
lassen to allow, let; to leave
laufen to run
leben to live
legen to lay
sich legen to lie down
leid tun to grieve, hurt
es tut mir leid I'm sorry
leiden to suffer; **ich kann ihn nicht leiden** I can't stand him
leihen to lend; **sich** (*dat*) **etw leihen** to borrow sth
leiten to guide, lead
lesen to read
lieben to love
liefern to deliver; to supply
liegen to be (situated)
loben to praise
löschen to put out
lösen to buy (*ticket*)
losmachen to unfasten, undo, untie

loswerden to get rid of
lügen to lie, tell a lie
machen to do; to make
malen to paint
meinen to think, believe
mieten to hire, rent
mitbringen to bring
mitnehmen to take
mitteilen: jdm etw mitteilen to inform sb of sth
mögen to like
murmeln to murmur
müssen to have to (*must*), be obliged to
nachdenken (über + *acc*) to think (about)
nachsehen to check
nähen to sew
sich nähern (+ *dat*) to approach
nehmen to take
nennen to call, name
sich niederlegen to go to bed, lie down
notieren to note
öffnen to open
organisieren to organize
passen (+ *dat*) to suit, be suitable
passieren to happen
pflegen to take care of
ich pflegte zu tun I used to do
plaudern to chat
pressen to press, squeeze
produzieren to produce
protestieren to protest
prüfen to examine, check
raten (+ *dat*) to advise

VERBS

räumen to clear away
reden to talk, speak
reinigen to clean, tidy up
reisen to go, travel
retten to save, rescue
riechen (nach) to smell (of)
rufen to call
sich rühren to stir
sagen (+ dat) to say (to), tell
säubern to clean
saugen to suck
schaden (+ dat) to harm
schallen to sound
schauen (auf + acc) to look
(at)
scheinen to seem; to shine
schieben to push, shove
schießen to shoot
schlafen to sleep
schlafen gehen to go to bed
schlagen to hit, strike,
knock, beat
sich schlagen to fight
(sich) schließen to close,
shut
schneiden to cut
schnüren to tie
schreiben to write
schreien to shout, cry
schütteln to shake
schützen (vor + dat) to
protect (from)
schweigen to be silent
schwören to swear
sehen to see
sein to be
senken to lower
setzen to put (down), place, set

sich setzen to settle, sit (down)
seufzen to sigh
singen to sing
sitzen to sit, be sitting
sollen ought (to)
sorgen für to take care of,
look after
sich sorgen (um) to worry
(about)
sparen to save
spaßen to joke
spazierengehen to go for a walk
sprechen to speak
stattfinden to take place
stecken to put, stick
stehen to stand
stehenbleiben to stop (still)
steigen to come or go up,
rise; to climb
stellen to put, place; to ask
(a question)
sterben to die
stimmen to be right
stoppen to stop (transitive)
stören to disturb
stoßen to push, shove
strecken to stretch
streiten to argue, fight
sich streiten to quarrel
stürzen to fall, crash
**sich stürzen (in or auf +
acc)** to rush or dash (into)
suchen to look for, search for
tanzen to dance
teilen to share, divide
teilnehmen (an + dat) to
attend, be present at, go to,
take part (in)
töten to kill

tragen to carry; to wear
träumen to dream
treffen to meet; to strike (*transitive*)
trennen to separate; to divide
treiben to drive; to go in for
trocknen to dry
tun to do
so tun, als ob to pretend (that)
überlegen to consider, reflect
überraschen to surprise
überreden to persuade
übersetzen to translate
(sich) umdrehen to turn round
umgeben (von) to surround (with *or* by)
umgehen to avoid, bypass
umkehren to turn
umleiten to divert
umwerfen to overturn, knock over
unterbrechen to interrupt
unterhalten to support
(sich) unterhalten (über + acc) to converse *or* talk (about); to entertain
sich unterscheiden to differ, be different
unterschreiben to sign
untersuchen to examine
sich verabreden to make an appointment
verbessern to improve
verbieten to forbid, prohibit
verbinden to connect; to bandage

verbringen to pass *or* spend (*time*)
verdecken to hide, cover up
verderben to spoil, ruin
verdienen to deserve
vereinigen to unite
vergessen to forget
sich verhalten to act, behave
verhindern to prevent
verlangen to demand, order
verlassen to leave
verleihen (an + acc) to lend (to)
verletzen to harm
verlieren to lose
es vermeiden, etw zu tun to avoid doing sth
vermieten to let, rent
versäumen to miss
(ver)schließen to lock
verschwinden to disappear, vanish
versehen (mit) to provide (with)
versichern (+ dat) to convince, assure
versprechen to promise
(sich) verstecken (vor + dat) to hide (from)
verstehen to understand; **was verstehen Sie darunter?** what do you understand by that?
versuchen to try, taste, sample; to attempt to
verteidigen to defend
verteilen to distribute
verzeihen to pardon, forgive

vollenden to finish
vorbereiten to prepare
vorgeben to pretend
vorschlagen to suggest
(sich) vorstellen to introduce (oneself)
sich (*dat*) **etw vorstellen** to imagine sth
wachen to be awake
wachsen to grow
wagen to dare
wählen to elect; to choose
warten (auf + *acc*) to wait (for)
(sich) waschen to wash
wechseln to exchange; to change (*money*)
wecken to awaken, wake up (*transitive*)
wegnehmen to take off *or* away
sich weigern to refuse
weinen to cry
sich wenden an (+ *acc*) to apply to; to turn (to)
werden to become, grow, turn (out)
werfen to throw
wetten (auf + *acc*) to bet (on)
wiederholen to repeat
wiedersehen to see again
wischen to wipe
wissen to know
wohnen (in + *dat*) to live (in)
wohnen (bei + *dat*) to lodge

(with), live (with)
wollen to want (to), wish (to)
sich wundern (über + *acc*) to wonder (at), be astonished (at *or* by)
es wundert mich I am surprised (at it)
das würde mich wundern! that would surprise me!
wünschen to wish
zählen to count
zeichnen to draw
zeigen to show, point
zelten to go camping
zerbrechen to break
zerreißen to tear up
zerstören to demolish, destroy
zerstreuen to scatter
ziehen to draw; to pull; to tug
zittern (vor) to tremble (with)
zögern to hesitate
zugeben to confess, admit
zuhören (+ *dat*) to listen (to)
zumachen to close, shut (*transitive*)
zurückkehren to come back, return
zurückkommen to go *or* come back
zurücksetzen, zurückstellen to replace
zweifeln to doubt
zwingen to force, oblige

The following German words have more than one translation, depending on context. If you do not already know all these translations, check them up on the pages shown.

das Alter 62, 81
der Anhänger 13, 42, 153, 191, 199
die Anmeldung 30, 204, 214
die Arbeit 32, 69
das Armaturenbrett 13, 42
der Ausdruck 51, 64
die Auskunft 11, 131, 136, 189
das Bad 123, 159
der Balkon 120, 124, 173
das Band 45, 99
die Bank 32, 131, 136, 154, 163
der Bauer 20, 84; das Bauer 20
der Becher 90, 150
der Berg 58, 76, 200
der Betrieb 34, 184
die Birne 102, 127
das Blatt 72, 192
der Boden 60, 85, 155
das Bord 107; der Bord 12, 159
das Brett 129, 180
der Briefkasten 126, 130
die Brücke 59, 129, 182, 189
die Büchse 31, 150
die Decke 124, 127
das Eis 93, 201
das Essen 30, 76, 204
die Fahrt 39, 182, 189
die Falte 47, 65

die Farbe 126, 163
die Feder 20, 181
die Figur 64, 174
das Fleisch 22, 93
die Fliege 46, 89
die Flut 161, 203
der Flügel 13, 21, 88, 145
die Frau 62, 81
der Gang 18, 40, 64, 74, 124
die Garderobe 73, 120, 174
der Gepäckträger 10, 18, 120, 191
das Gericht 96, 137
das Geschirr 31, 87, 96, 127
das Geschäft 33, 164, 183
das Glas 140, 150
der Grund 58, 154, 216
die Größe 45, 62, 163
der Hahn 20, 127
die Handlung 163, 172
die Heide 60, 85
die Hütte 155, 155
die Kapelle 144, 175, 216
die Karte 69, 172
die Kasse 131, 163, 172
der Kiefer 24; die Kiefer, pl -n 192
das Konzert 144, 172
das Kostüm 46, 174
die Küche 122, 204
der Laden 125, 162, 182
das Land 58, 76, 84, 201
die Leinwand 143, 175
der Leiter 36; die Leiter,

The vocabulary lists on the following pages cover all of the nouns in the first two levels of the book, i.e. ESSENTIAL and IMPORTANT, and will be a useful translation guide when you have a mental blank.